Praise for

How to Act Right When Your Spouse Acts Wrong

"Leslie has hit the nail on the head. She masterfully weaves together God's purpose for marriage and gently encourages us to become all God calls us to within the joys and hardships of that relationship. We applaud Leslie's stand in a world of quick fixes and dissolving marriages. She reminds us that marriage isn't about finding the right person but becoming the right person."

—FRED AND FLORENCE LITTAUER,
Christian Leaders, Authors & Speakers Services, Inc.

"A fresh and practical approach to seemingly insurmountable problems! Leslie does not offer easy answers for couples in crisis—she offers Christ and assurance that, indeed, He is enough."

—BECKY FREEMAN, author of *Chocolate Chili Pepper Love*
and *Marriage 911*

How
to Act
Right

When Your
Spouse Acts
Wrong

How
to Act
Right

When Your
Spouse Acts
Wrong

Leslie Vernick

WATERBROOK
PRESS

HOW TO ACT RIGHT WHEN YOUR SPOUSE ACTS WRONG
PUBLISHED BY WATERBROOK PRESS
12265 Oracle Boulevard, Suite 200
Colorado Springs, Colorado 80921

All Scripture quotations, unless otherwise indicated, are taken from the Holy Bible,
New International Version®. NIV®. Copyright © 1973, 1978, 1984 by International Bible
Society. Used by permission of Zondervan Publishing House. All rights reserved. Scripture
quotations marked (msg) are taken from The Message. Copyright © by Eugene H. Peterson
1993, 1994, 1995. Used by permission of NavPress Publishing Group.

Any italics in Scripture quotes are the author's.

Some of the stories in this book are composites of several different situations; details
and names have been changed to protect identities.

ISBN 978-0-307-45849-0
ISBN 978-0-307-45751-6 (electronic)

Published in the United States by WaterBrook Multnomah, an imprint of the Crown
Publishing Group, a division of Random House Inc., New York.

WATERBROOK and its deer colophon are registered trademarks of Random House Inc.

Library of Congress Cataloging-in-Publication Data
Vernick, Leslie.
    How to act right when your spouse acts wrong / Leslie Vernick.— 1st ed.
      p. cm.
      1. Spouses—Religious life. 2. Marriage—Religious aspects—Christianity. I. Title.
BV4596.M3 V47 2001
248.8'44—dc21

                                                                      2001026280

Printed in the United States of America
2013

10 9 8 7

SPECIAL SALES
Most WaterBrook Multnomah books are available at special quantity discounts when
purchased in bulk by corporations, organizations, and special-interest groups. Custom
imprinting or excerpting can also be done to fit special needs. For information, please
e-mail SpecialMarkets@WaterBrookMultnomah.com or call 1-800-603-7051.

To Howard,

who acts right when I act wrong—most of the time

CONTENTS

Contents

FOREWORD

Nearly half of today's marriages will end in divorce. But that statistic doesn't do justice to the true number of couples suffering the heartbreak of love gone bad. For all the people in the throes of separation and divorce, there are millions more married individuals who are living in their own private worlds of pain. Their hearts cry out, "All I've ever wanted is for someone to love me."

Some of the most painful situations occur when one spouse desperately wants to fix what is broken, but the other is stuck in a pattern of destructive behavior and apparently has no intention of changing. This creates a painful dilemma for the spouse who wants to do the right thing and remain committed to God and his or her marriage vows.

The answers and guidance we give these individuals has often been woefully inadequate. Are the only alternatives to leave the marriage or to accept the situation and withdraw into painful isolation? No. In this book Leslie Vernick tackles this delicate and challenging dilemma with wisdom and compassion. She offers practical advice, profound truth, and hope-filled alternatives for those in seemingly hopeless situations. Change begins with us as we search our own hearts before God and seek to be defined by love.

This book will help restore a sense of power to those who feel powerless. Leslie helps us walk through life proactively, not reactively. We do have the power to make choices, the power to grow, to forgive, to love, and to do the right thing—even if our partner continues to do the wrong thing.

—DR. TIM CLINTON
President, American Association of Christian Counselors

WORDS OF THANKS

This book could not have been written without the many people who have allowed me to walk by their side during some of the most difficult times of their lives. Thank you from the bottom of my heart for the privilege of being a part of your healing process. Whenever I used an example from my counseling practice, identifying information and details have been altered so that your confidentiality will be protected. In some cases I have blended various stories because they were so similar. I trust you will be encouraged that the pain you've experienced might be used in some way to help others.

If you are struggling because your spouse is acting wrong or not acting as you'd like, my prayer is that by reading this book, you will begin to see that God is at work, even if your spouse doesn't change. There are great blessings for you and your children if you will learn what God is teaching you through these tough times. I have been witness again and again to the life-changing power of God's Word to bring hope and healing, and my desire is that you, too, will find renewal and strength to stay the course of becoming more like Jesus.

Many thanks go out to my dear friends and colleagues who prayed, supported, and sharpened me while writing this book. To Georgia Shaffer, Glenna Dameron, John Bettler, and my pastor, Howard Lawler—I appreciate the time you took to comb through the first draft of my manuscript and lend your valuable insights and comments. Theresa Cain, a kindred spirit and true friend, thank you for your love and your labor of prayer for the birthing of this book. Dave and Barb Schindler, thanks for generously providing the absolute best place to write—your oceanfront beach house. Bless you.

Writing a book also takes its toll on the family. I am so grateful for my husband, Howard, and our children, Ryan and Amanda, who support and encourage the gifts God has given me and want me to use them to the fullest. Thank you for being sensitive and patient, willing to help fill in the gaps on the home front when necessary.

To WaterBrook Press and especially Erin Healy, my editor and friend, thanks for believing in this project and in my ability to bring it to pass. Without a doubt your encouragement and affirmation have enlarged me.

Last, but certainly not least, God, every day you amaze me. Thank you for the privilege of knowing and serving you.

INTRODUCTION

This book is important for every married person—or those who are about to be married. All of us at one time or another face the dilemma of choosing to act right when our spouse acts wrong.

Whenever our spouse disappoints us, fails us, hurts us, or just plain irritates us, whether in big ways or little ways, *from our perspective* he or she is wrong.

Sin is in all of us (Romans 3:23). Attitudes and behaviors that come out of a self-centered, selfish, prideful, deceived, and/or rebellious heart often express themselves in big, bad ways such as infidelity, lying, addictions, or abuse. The same sinful heart can also produce more benign but chronically irritating behaviors such as nagging and criticism, forgetting important occasions, failing to put dirty laundry in the hamper, not listening well, or staying glued to the television when our spouse is attempting to have a conversation with us. It can be just as difficult and discouraging to believe God and live by faith with a spouse who sins in subtle, less blatant ways as it can when a spouse commits the more grievous wrongs.

Most of us acknowledge that there are no perfect marriages or perfect spouses. We know that having a good marriage requires effort and hard work. At times, however, in the midst of that pain and struggle we can lose sight of what marriage is all about. We forget that we have made a covenant promise to love for better or worse. In the better times, love is usually easy. When worse comes, we often don't know *how* to continue to love when we are angry, hurt, scared, or don't *feel* very loving. We also aren't exactly sure what that kind of love is supposed to look like. Do we just forbear? Forgive and forget? How and when do we apply the bolder forms of love?

Research shows that we aren't doing very well with this struggle. Currently, the national divorce rate is slightly higher for those who claim to be "born again" than for the general population.[1] Each day in my counseling practice I work with Christians who struggle in marriages that are unhappy or problematic. Ending a marriage that one finds difficult or unsatisfying is a real temptation. Christians opt for that path with increasing frequency even though they know, in most cases, that God desires them to stay in their marriage and work out the difficulties. Others stay married but in name only. Their hearts are cold toward their spouse and toward God, whom they think has ordered them to stay in a marriage they find too difficult.

Surely there must be a better alternative. In *How to Act Right When Your Spouse Acts Wrong*, you will begin to see yourself and your marriage through the lens of God's eternal purposes. You will learn how God uses the imperfections, differences, and sins of your spouse to help *you* grow to be more like Christ. This book will help you learn *how* to love and to *keep* your promises when it is hard. When you don't feel like it. When you are not getting much in return. And probably most important, this book will show you why this is good for you to learn.

It's been said that marriage isn't about finding the right person but about becoming the right person. I am humbled by the reality that I am still learning to be the kind of wife God calls me to be and the kind of wife my husband needs. I don't always act right or do right, especially when my husband disappoints me or fails me. But in the twenty-five years we have shared, I have learned to do it better and more consistently. Like some of you, I, too, have a long way to go, but I have gained some personal and professional wisdom over the years that may help make your journey more successful.

Unfortunately, these days I meet many who aren't looking for deep personal change or growth. Instead, they want a quick fix or relief from pain. People often say to me, "Just tell me what I can do to make this better—*now!*" I recently gave a seminar on the subject of how to make your marriage happier. At the conclusion of my talk, audiotapes and books were available for those who were interested. Every item that dealt with ways to make yourself or your marriage happier was snapped up in minutes. Tapes and books about the deeper life and attaining spiritual growth and maturity were left behind. Those subjects were less appealing to that crowd, yet God tells us that deepening our relationship with him is the very cornerstone to our well-being and happiness.

Learning to respond rightly when we are wronged and wounded takes maturity and wisdom—and hard work. God is interested in developing the character of Christ within us. Merely learning some tricks or techniques will not be enough to deal with the heart issues that rise to the surface of our lives when our spouse doesn't act in the way we desire. Although the quick fix looks appealing, many of us have already learned (often the hard way) that the path that appears easiest turns out to be the more difficult in the long run.

Maturity and growth usually take place in the context of relationships. Right from the beginning of life, God places us into a family.

Within this environment of family interaction we begin to experience love and conflict, joy and sadness, intimacy and alienation. Our parents help shape our character (in both positive and negative ways). We begin to define who we are to a large extent by how we interact with others. Are we kind? loyal? selfish? helpful? Do we think of others or only of ourselves? The people in our family help shape us, and our interaction with them exposes us. We can't pretend for long in the context of family. Conflicts, pain, disappointment, and anger often rip off our pleasant exterior persona and expose our uglier side.

If we have come to Christ through a conversion experience, we also have an interactive relationship with him. He gives us a new identity and purpose. He loves us with an everlasting love. He adopts us as his children, and he seeks to shape our character to become more and more like his. But that's not all. He puts us into another family—the family of God. His Word instructs us how to treat one another, even when we are being treated unfairly. The daily environment of family life, both in the church and in our homes, reveals our weaknesses and sins. Although this is painful, it is ultimately a good thing. When we are exposed, we cannot deceive ourselves into thinking that we are something we are not. Exposure shows us (often in bold colors) the areas where we don't trust God fully and where God wants us to yield ourselves to him so that we might become more like Jesus.

When we speak of acting "right," we must be careful not to think that what looks like the right response for a person with one type of marital difficulties is always the *right* response for another. When attempting to apply Scripture to life's troubles, many of us often reduce it to a rule book. It is much easier to have pat answers for all of life's difficulties. Yet life is not that simple, and God's Word is much richer than just a set of rules to live by. For example, some women have believed that when their husband mistreats them physically, emotionally, or sexually, they should obey God and become more like Christ by yielding to the abuse as an act of submission. One woman who had been taught this thought that Jesus wanted her to be "led like a lamb to the slaughter." Perhaps acting right or acting like Christ in this marriage might involve a deeper and more accurate understanding of submission and headship. For this particular woman, loving her husband or acting right may require speaking up respectfully yet boldly against the evil in their marital relationship. It might mean she must learn to speak the truth about how God sees her husband's abusive behavior and how it is destroying their marriage. It may even involve exposing the deeds of darkness to others and allowing her spouse to experience the consequences of his sin in order to bring him to the possibility of repentance. I will be saying more in chapter 9 on how to respond correctly to the more difficult and sensitive marital problems.

To take this idea a step farther, what's right in one situation may be wrong in another. Someone whose spouse commits a grievous sin against him or her may need to speak up and boldly enforce consequences for destructive behaviors. On the other hand, many of us blurt out what we think our spouse is doing wrong without much thought or any prayer. Acting right may involve keeping quiet at times and accepting our spouse's weakness. Too often we take a cookie-cutter approach to solving marital difficulties and try to make answers that fit one type of problem work for a completely different situation. We would never respect a doctor who treated each patient the same way with the same surgical procedure or medication for every ailment. Neither can we take such a naive approach in learning to act right when our spouse acts wrong. Yet in all situations, God's Word calls us to holy actions bathed in loving attitudes.

Today we live in a culture that is more concerned with getting than giving. Over and over again in my counseling sessions I hear spouses complain, "My needs aren't being met in my marriage." Dissatisfaction, anger, resentment, and bitterness are the mainstays in many homes because we go into marriage seeking what we can get out of it. Acting right when our spouse acts wrong will not necessarily guarantee a more satisfying marital relationship, although it often does. Acting right may not make our spouse turn around and change his or her ways or meet our needs, although it could. God says that we exert a powerful influence over others as we seek to lovingly interact with them. (See 1 Thessalonians 5:11; Hebrews 10:24-25; Proverbs 27:17.)

As we start learning how to act right when our spouse acts wrong, we will begin to see what God is doing to make us more like him in the midst of marital difficulties. We will become able to look at the idiosyncratic differences of our spouse less problematically and learn how to respond wisely when wronged. Perhaps most important of all, learning to act right when our spouse acts wrong will force us to forage for a deeper relationship with Christ. For to act right with a pure and sincere heart in the midst of suffering will stretch our faith and trust in God as we struggle to yield our will to his plan for our life.

The marriage relationship is a picture of our covenant relationship with Christ. He is going to be our teacher in this process, for he always acts right.

Even when we act wrong.

ONE

WHY BOTHER TO ACT RIGHT?

*May I view and long after holiness
as the beauty and dignity of the soul.*

FROM A PURITAN PRAYER

David barely squeezed his large frame snugly between the arms of my chair in my office. His eyes brimming with tears, he poured out his pain. "I've tried everything, Leslie. For the past two years, I've read books on how to be a good husband, a godly man, and an effective father. I've gone to PromiseKeepers, Bible studies, and my pastor for help. But it isn't working and I'm so tired. My wife, Julie, still doesn't want anything to do with me. I feel like giving up. Nothing is happening."

David's heart is breaking. His marriage is in trouble, and he's not sure if anything he can do will ever change it to be what he desires. David expresses the sorrow of many who see nothing in their marriage change even when they have tried to act right when their spouse acts wrong. They try hard, often with marathon efforts, but their spouse doesn't respond the way they hope. Their marriage is still distant, painful, full of conflict, or superficially pleasant but emotionally cold. David believed God would change his spouse *if only* he learned to act right.

Isn't that what we've been taught? If we do the right thing, then our marriage *will* get better. Carrie thought so. Her husband had an affair with a coworker. When Sam confessed it, she tried to respond in the right way. She went to counseling, expressed her feelings, forgave her husband, and in every way attempted to reconcile her marriage. Her husband even agreed to come home. Then they found out his coworker was pregnant. The bitter irony was that Carrie and Sam had tried unsuccessfully to have children. Sam divorced Carrie and married the other woman. Carrie was devastated. She had tried with all her heart to do it right. What happened? Hadn't God promised to give her the desires of her heart? Carrie felt God had let her down.

Over the years I have heard variations of these stories again and again. We pray hard and read our Bible and other books, trying this or that, looking expectantly for our spouse to soften, change, forgive us, or repent. When that doesn't happen, like David or Carrie, we can become angry, discouraged, and disillusioned. We are tempted to give up on our marriage—and sometimes on our faith—and conclude that God and his principles are impotent. We think, *Why bother? It won't do any good anyway!*

Perhaps that's why you've picked up this book. Perhaps you are still looking for the technique that will improve your marriage. You want something—anything—to make your spouse change or to turn your marriage into something more like what God says it should be. These desires are good and legitimate, and all of us who are married have them. Often as we grow and learn how to love our husband or wife in more Christlike ways, our spouse notices, responds positively, and our marriage does improve. But sometimes it doesn't.

David's comment rang true. Nothing significant *was* changing in his marriage. Julie was still angry with him over some old wounds he'd inflicted years earlier. She was still unresponsive sexually and not interested in working either on her own attitude or their marriage. *So why continue trying?* David wondered. *And what am I trying for?* Just like David, we might conclude nothing is happening.

Or is it?

Acting Right When Our Spouse Acts Wrong Is Good for Us

These painful kinds of experiences often cause us to begin asking God some important questions. Most of the time, we start by asking him a lot of *why* questions. *Why is this happening to me? Why should I bother trying when there doesn't seem to be any marital improvement or change in my spouse?* Talking with God about our troubles is good, and he welcomes a heart that seeks to understand his purposes. Jesus always responded to others' questions, especially those that came from people who were genuinely looking for truth. When God gives us his answers, however, we may not always like what he tells us.

As most children do, I often asked my father, "Why?" Why couldn't I stay out until one o'clock in the morning? Why did I have to stay home and work around the house? His two favorite responses were "Because I said so" and "Because it's good for you." I never liked either one of those answers much. From my point of view, they were inadequate explanations. I always thought he said those things to get out of having to give me a real answer. Yet over the years (in part because I have become a parent myself) I have found profound truths in each of my father's short responses.

The first one, "Because I said so," implies authority. Who is the "I" in that answer? It isn't just anybody who said so. It was my father who said so. Imagine one of your friends asking you to do something. When you question her about it, she replies, "Because I said so." What would be your reaction? I'd laugh aloud, or I might even be bold enough to say with a twinkle in my eye, "And who are you?" When my father said "Because I said so," the statement assumed his authority and my need to trust and obey him, not because I understood him or agreed with him, but because he was my father. Perhaps he knew that I was too immature, too foolish, or too rebellious at the time to grasp the wisdom behind his decisions. I wasn't going to get it just then. I would simply have to choose whether I would trust his judgment and obey him.

Throughout God's Word, people ask God why, and sometimes he responds just as my father did—"Because I said so." (See, for example, Isaiah 45:5-12.) This phrase is not the trite response of a God who has no better explanation. It is an answer overflowing with truth. It directs our attention away from our problem and toward the One who has the power and the authority to orchestrate the details of our lives. At times God uses our circumstances to make us more aware of him. Instead of asking why, we begin to ask, "Who is this One?" God understands our deeper need in the situation. It isn't to know more of *why;* rather, it is to know more of *him.*

Job experienced this transformation. After Job lost his children, his wealth, and his health, he asked God why. He didn't understand. What had he done to deserve this kind of hardship, this kind of hurt? Throughout Job's ordeal, he never lost his faith, but he did get more and more insistent upon an answer to his question. After a very long silence, God answered Job—but not with the answer Job wanted. God replied to Job with a long series of his own questions, in essence asking Job, "Are you God? Can you know all things? Do all things? Be all things?" (See Job 38-41.) God finally cornered Job: "Will the one who contends with the Almighty correct him? Let him who accuses God answer him!" (Job 40:2). Job began to grasp the moment. Instead of looking for answers, he was now looking at God. In stunned silence he covered his mouth with his hand. Job's transformation began, and instead of demanding answers from God, Job worshiped him.

Sometimes in the midst of our marital pain and confusion, God moves us toward a greater knowledge and a deeper experience of him. It is often in the middle of our search for the answer to why that he begins to redirect our attention. Instead of asking why, we turn and start asking God *what*. What can we learn about God and our life from this experience? We ask God for a stronger faith to believe him and to trust and obey him even when we don't understand. We also begin to ask if there is a greater purpose for our life other than marital bliss and a happy family life. We want to understand what God might be doing in us through our difficult marital relationship.

This leads us to the second answer my father gave: "Because it's good for you." Whenever I heard this I would cringe. I looked on this explanation with great suspicion, because what was good for me was usually unpleasant. I remember my own children kicking and screaming when they had to go to the pediatrician's office for their checkups, because the visits often involved getting some sort of shot. Equally distasteful was the dentist. Yet I would have been an irresponsible parent if I had neglected medical and dental care just because my children couldn't grasp that regular visits were good for them. Contrary to what they believed at the time, I found no pleasure in torturing them. I knew my children would never volunteer to go to the doctor or dentist. I made them go. Why? It was good for them.

When God says something is for our good, what does this mean? Often we hope it means that God will eventually bring happiness or pleasure out of a difficult situation. But just as my children never had any pleasure or happiness in their visits to the dentist, sometimes we do not experience any happiness or pleasure in the things God says are good for us. Many things that we instinctively find unappealing are indeed good for us. Hebrews 12 says that discipline seems unpleasant for the moment, but when we have been trained by it, it will yield the fruit of righteousness. So what does God mean when he says he uses and sometimes even causes difficult situations for our good?

Some of you might be thinking, *Wait a minute! Are you saying that when my spouse acts wrong, God uses that for my good? Surely God didn't want Julie to act that way toward her husband, David.* You are right. Julie definitely could have made better choices when she became hurt early in her marriage. Julie could have chosen to act right when David acted wrong. She didn't. Instead, she allowed her anger to fester until it eventually hardened into a solid rock of bitterness, indifference, and apathy toward David. Now the tables were turned, and Julie was acting wrong. She was not loving. She was not forgiving. How could God use *that* for good in David's life?

As sinful human beings, we are always tempted to first point the finger at our spouse when we think he or she is acting wrong. David tried that. He told Julie she was bitter. She needed to forgive him. He wanted her to feel bad, guilty, embarrassed—anything but this cold indifference that he could not penetrate. It didn't work. That's when he began trying to change himself into a more loving husband. He bought her flowers, cleaned up the dishes, invited her out for romantic dinners, and bought her some special jewelry that she had admired. David's approach to Julie had changed, *but his motives hadn't*. David's new behaviors may have looked more loving, but his heart was still motivated by his own desire to see Julie change. We might fool others with that kind of outward change, but we will never fool our spouse. David's selfishness came out in a hundred less obvious, less demanding ways than it had in the past. Even so, he was only acting more loving *so that Julie would change*. He wanted her to love him.

David's agenda from the beginning of his marriage was the selfish desire to turn Julie into the wife he wanted. Many of their early problems were rooted in this mind-set. He wanted her to love him, meet his needs, care for him. When she failed he scolded her. He withdrew from her. He often sulked and pouted. Finally Julie had enough and became angry. This startled David. While dating, Julie accommodated his every wish and desire. Her primary concern was his happiness. Now she ignored him. First David tried waiting for her to get over her anger. That didn't happen. Next he tried asserting his authority as her husband and ordered her to meet his needs, which only fueled Julie's hurt and resentment. Finally, in desperation, he tried the loving approach, attempting to rewin her heart. Still Julie didn't respond as he wanted. Although things were less hostile between them, nothing was changing in their marital relationship. Well, almost nothing. Something was very definitely happening in these difficult years, but it wasn't in David's marriage.

It was happening in him.

God's Purpose for Marriage

I have an acquaintance who collects Martin guitars. These guitars are among the finest in the world. They are handmade by expert craftsmen not far from my home in Pennsylvania. What a Steinway is to a piano, a Martin is to a guitar. A Martin's purpose and function is to resonate with beautiful, rich melodies when played by an expert guitarist. Yet my friend is not a musician and does not play his guitars. Instead, he frames them and hangs them on his walls.

Now I must admit they do look striking in their glass boxes hanging on his walls, but that is not what they were designed for. Those beautiful handmade guitars are falling far short of their intended purpose. Guitars could be used as tables for holding drinks or as weapons for hitting others! Guitars can function in a variety of different ways, but the purpose of their design is to make music.

Most of us get married because we believe we have found the right person with whom to share our life. We choose someone whom we think will care for us and meet our needs for companionship, love, and sexual intimacy. Although these are important ingredients in any happy marriage, are they God's ultimate purpose for marriage? What if marriage wasn't designed primarily for our happiness but to teach us holiness?[1] Remember, most of our emotional and spiritual growth takes place in the context of our relationships. Could it be that God uses the marital relationship to help us mature, to become more like Christ? (See also Hebrews 12:14.)

Is it possible that God was using David's marital troubles (specifically Julie's acting wrong) to teach him to be a godly husband? How would the Lord accomplish this? First, he would need to expose the self-centeredness that oriented much of David's behaviors. What happened *to* David and *in* David when he realized his wife wasn't the wife he had hoped for? As David and I talked, he began to acknowledge that he married Julie primarily to meet his felt needs. If we are honest, we all have to admit to having this as a primary motive for marriage.

God uses the marital relationship as a picture of Christ and his bride, the church. Christ gives himself to meet our *real* and *true* needs, not just our felt needs. He never demands that his needs be met in return. Within the intimacy of the marital relationship we can learn to express this kind of sacrificial loving and giving (Ephesians 5:25).

By nature, we are more concerned with being served than serving, with getting rather than giving. Self-sacrifice, suffering, and servanthood are subjects rarely taught in any premarital counseling class. Most of us avoid these topics like the plague. Within the context of David's marital troubles, God was schooling him in a practical sense on what it means to die to self.

Something indeed was happening *in* David through his troubled marriage. God was teaching David personal lessons on *how* to grow and to become more and more like Jesus. God was teaching David *how* to be more loving, even when Julie didn't love him in return. He was teaching David *how* to forgive, even when Julie never apologized. He was showing David *how* he could overcome evil with good and *how* to be content in all things. These lessons are not learned from a book or in the context of marital bliss, but in hardship.

In addition, God wanted David to understand the suffering of Christ. Jesus was rejected. So was David. Jesus was up against hard-hearted and stubborn people. So was David. Jesus loved and served, gave and sacrificed, often getting nothing in return. So did David. David would never fully mature and be like Christ as long as his own legitimate desires (to have a good marriage, to have Julie forgive him and love him in return) controlled him. Through David's marital troubles, God was working to build the character of Jesus into him. The apostle Paul encourages us that the love and peace of Christ is to rule us, not our own heartfelt desires. (See Colossians 3:15 and 2 Corinthians 5:14.) David needed to learn *how* to find his joy and happiness in God and not in his wife, even though he still longed for a loving companion.

Why was David suffering in a difficult marriage? We don't know all the answers, but perhaps one of the answers God gives is that it is good for him. "Marriage is more than a sacred covenant with another person. It is a spiritual discipline designed to help you know God better, trust him more fully, and love him more deeply."[2]

Felt Needs Versus Real Needs

Learning to discern the difference between our felt needs and our real needs takes us over tricky terrain. Our felt needs *feel* so real and necessary to our well-being and happiness, while our real needs often sit on the back burner, unattended for years. For example, every day I feel a need for a little chocolate. Okay, a lot of chocolate. My body craves chocolate, but my *real* need is to eat a more healthy diet and to forsake my chocolate for some broccoli or a banana. Often I feel a need for praise, admiration, appreciation, or gratitude from someone I have been serving, but perhaps my *real* need is to develop humility, meekness, and selflessness. God gives us our spouse as a helpmate—to meet our needs. Is he or she used by God primarily to meet our *real* needs, or just our *felt* needs? Oswald Chambers asks, "If I could look at myself from God's perspective, what would I see as my true needs?"[3]

When we allow God to define our true needs, we can learn to trust him even when we don't understand our difficulties. We learn that when our spouse acts wrong and we feel hurt or wounded, lonely or unloved, ignored or mistreated, taken for granted or taken to the cleaners, God uses something about that experience to bring us into a deeper relationship with him and greater maturity in our lives. To believe this, we must see our marriage as something far more important than just a venue where our felt needs will be met; rather, we must see our marriage as an opportunity to depend on God to meet our real needs. It was while the apostle Paul was in prison, in a state of deprivation where felt needs were concerned, that he penned the familiar words, "My God will meet all your needs according to his glorious riches in Christ Jesus" (Philippians 4:19).

It Is Good for Your Marriage

It is good for you to learn to act right when your spouse acts wrong because doing so will help you grow in your relationship with

Christ. Acting right is also good for your marriage. Things in a home deteriorate quickly when two sinners continue sinning at the same time.

Recently I had been acting crabby because of deadlines and pressures related to my work. I wasn't sensitive to my husband, Howard, and was fully wrapped up in my own agenda. In addition to that, I criticized him for not being more helpful around the house. Instead of reacting defensively or argumentatively, he simply asked what he could do to help. Then he took it upon himself to plan the entire menu for the coming week (hot dogs, chicken patties, frozen pizza, and so on), do the grocery shopping, and prepare the meals each evening. Although the meals were simple, the love behind it was extravagant. It is an incredible gift to our spouse and to our marriage when we choose to act right even when our spouse acts wrong.

Joanna decided to come to me for marital counseling, even though her husband refused to accompany her. Joanna chose not to let that deter her from working on herself, including areas that her husband complained about. Her goal in counseling wasn't to please her husband or necessarily to improve her marriage, but to know God better and to grow to be more like Jesus.

Joanna has faithfully worked on the things God has shown her about herself, such as her stubbornness, her critical spirit, her haughtiness, and her fear and anxiety. Over the months she has learned to pray and to study her Bible so that she knows that God is talking with her as she reads it. Her husband has never attended a counseling session nor asked her what she works on. Yet recently she said to me, "Leslie, my marriage isn't perfect, but it's the best it has ever been." Taking the time to work on yourself so that you grow and learn to become a better spouse doesn't *guarantee* a better marriage, but it sure doesn't hurt.

It Is Good for Your Spouse

In my book *The TRUTH Principle* I tell of a couple, Jack and Mary, who had marital troubles. Jack was always angry, very controlling, and somewhat abusive. Mary was just the opposite: timid, fearful, and a pleaser by nature. As long as Mary did everything Jack wanted, their relationship went smoothly. If Mary failed, she always had a price to pay. Mary thought a good Christian wife should always give in and submit to her husband's demands. However, as she and I worked together, she saw that this perspective was ultimately not in Jack's best interests. She was feeding a monster. The more she gave in to him, the more demanding and controlling he became. Mary needed to learn how to act right, which, in her case, was by speaking up about Jack's sinful behaviors, not by giving in. Mary needed to learn how to clearly speak the truth in love, confront her husband's behaviors, and set appropriate boundaries. As she learned to do this, Jack tried to get Mary to go back to her old ways. At first, his anger and intimidation worsened. Mary stayed firm in her resolve to love Jack by acting in his best interests and not giving in to him. Mary's new behaviors functioned as a mirror that gave Jack an accurate reflection of what he was like to live with. Through the changes in her, he began to recognize his own selfishness and sinful anger. This was good for Jack. It gave him, too, the opportunity to make some changes, which, in this case, he ultimately did.

It Is Good for Your Children

Children are often the innocent causalities of war—at home. Our children learn from us how to treat one another. God makes it plain how we Christians should treat one another, even those who position themselves as our enemies.

Adam and Celia often had knock-down-drag-out verbal wars in front of their two children. One would start with a critical or smart comment, the other would throw a remark back, and soon they would be off, back and forth, tit for tat, blow for blow. Each was determined not to be outdone by the other. Often these verbal wars would occur in the car, where their children were a captive audience. Later, in chapter 3, I will discuss how to avoid reacting to this kind of provocative situation. For the time being, understand that when you treat your spouse sinfully, especially in front of your children, you teach them how to behave toward others when they feel angry or upset. Don't be surprised if they start treating you in the same disrespectful ways they have observed you treating your husband or wife.

At times we may feel real hatred toward our mate. Our spouse may have betrayed us in the most horrific ways, and the temptation to disparage his or her character to our children is real. Sometimes in the midst of our own pain, we want to strike back. We want to hurt our spouse; turning our children's hearts against him or her is one way to do that. We may also be tempted to use our children's natural compassion to garner emotional support and may lean on them inappropriately as confidants or sounding boards.

Children need both parents, even if one of them has been a rotten spouse. "The empirical evidence is abundantly clear: *Kids get the best deal when they are raised in two-parent, married households*. Period."[4] Children are not stupid. They can see for themselves the shortcomings or sins of their parents. They don't need us to identify them. Yet children also have the remarkable ability to continue to love us as parents even when they know we have failed.

When I was eight years old, my mother decided she no longer wanted to be married to my father and divorced him. I have many ugly memories of that time during my childhood. Yet I have no recollection of my father slandering my mother. Only after I became an adult did he tell me his side of the story. I think that was a kindness. Children are not equipped to deal with the sordid details of their parents' sinfulness.

It Pleases God

It is good to learn to act right when our spouse acts wrong because it pleases God. In fact, it thrills him when we believe what he tells us, when we trust him even though it is hard.

When Abram believed God, it was counted to him as righteousness (Genesis 15:6). Jesus marveled at the faith of Gentiles that surpassed the faith of the Jews (Luke 7:9). The apostle Paul encourages us to grow in faith and appreciation of all God has done for us so our attitudes and behaviors will more and more reflect those of Jesus. God was well pleased with Christ's obedience (see John 8:29; Philippians 2; Ephesians 5), and he is likewise pleased with ours.

As a child, I longed for my parents' recognition and approval. At times I worked hard, not because I wanted to or thought it was a good idea, but just to hear the words "Good job. I'm proud of you." Some of us have never heard those precious words, or perhaps we didn't hear them often enough. Others heard just the opposite: "You're never good enough" or "What's wrong with you?" We still long for the blessing or approval from one or both of our parents. We want to hear them say they are proud of us or that they love us.

As God's children, one of the most heart-thrilling pronouncements we will ever hear our Father make will be, "Well done, good and faithful servant" (Matthew 25:23; see 2 Peter 1:11). Imagine the shame of seeing what our life could have been if we had only believed and trusted God instead of trying to make things work in our own strength or in our own wisdom. Again, it is good to learn to act right when our spouse (or, for that matter, anyone else) acts wrong toward us, because it pleases God that we would learn this, that we would even desire to learn it. Yet many of us feel stuck, unable to grasp a vision for our growth during difficulties, because our thoughts focus more on our own agenda rather than on God's.

Mental Obstacles that Hinder God's Plan for Our Maturity

"It's not fair! Why should I have to work on things when my spouse won't?"
Most of us live under the illusion that life is fair—or at least *should* be. The illusion that marriage is fifty-fifty. I shouldn't have to give more

than I get. This kind of wishful thinking will always keep us stuck in immaturity or resentment. Or both.

Jill wanted Ted to pitch in around the house. After all, they both worked full-time, and she couldn't understand why he wouldn't take half the responsibility for their household tasks. She nagged, she criticized, she complained, she sulked, she begged, but nothing changed. Ted would make halfhearted attempts for a time but always fell back into his old patterns. Keeping a clean and orderly house was just not as important to Ted as it was to Jill. Relaxing and enjoying fun activities during his off-hours were higher priorities. Jill was furious.

"Why should I have to do it?" she cried. "It's not fair." Jill is right. It's not fair that Ted won't at least take on a fair share of household duties, especially since he enjoys living in a large house that requires some maintenance. Jill, however, is the one who will stay stuck if she *has* to have Ted's help or fairness in her marriage in order for her to be happy. She will never be able to become the woman Jesus wants her to be if she is always busy keeping a scorecard, trying to ensure that she and Ted are making equal contributions to their marriage.

God never promises us that life is fair, that we will get as much as we give, or that our spouse will change if we act right or do right. Every marriage produces some sort of suffering, because when we don't get what we want, we suffer in big ways and in little ways. Because it is most difficult to act right in the midst of suffering, we will have to decide how we will respond to our discomfort. Will it be with anger, pouting, retaliation, or withdrawal, or will it be with the gentleness and kindness of Jesus? Could it be that God is using Ted's behavior to conform Jill to the image of Christ?

If we lose sight of the goal—Christlikeness—we will become frustrated in our attempts to act right when our spouse acts wrong. Our purpose in learning to act right is *not* to get our spouse to act right, to be fair, or to contribute more to the marriage. We cannot control our spouse's heart. With our goal set on pleasing God and being more like Jesus in all circumstances, we will begin to grow and to know the mind of Christ.

"What about me?"

Darlene decided to separate from Jonathan, her husband of twenty-five years. "I'm just so bored with him. I should never have married him. We are totally incompatible. He never wants to improve himself. All he does is watch TV. The kids are grown, and now it's time for me to discover who I am." Darlene found new friends at work and refused to talk with her husband about working to reconcile their marriage.

Darlene's dissatisfaction with her marriage is understandable. After twenty-five years of giving herself to raising her children and to serving a husband who rarely talked to her, it makes sense that she now wants time to think of herself. Although logical, any approach that leads us to look out for or "find" *our self* merits caution. No one is more interested in our personhood than Jesus. That's why we must never strike out on our own, leaving him out of the process, to go in search of our self. In fact, he warns us, "Whoever finds his life will lose it, but whoever loses his life for my sake will find it" (Matthew 10:39). Note that this verse doesn't say when we lose our life we will find Christ; rather, it says when we lose our life for Christ's sake, we will end up finding *our life*.

Darlene's pain was real, but had she chosen to act differently in response to her hardship, her pain may have led her toward Christ and a deeper appreciation of his suffering. Instead she chose to cut him out of her life so that she would not feel guilty about leaving her husband. Jesus tells us, "I have come that they may have life, and have it to the full" (John 10:10). Too often we hear these verses over and over but don't really grasp their meaning. No one's true self can be found apart from God; it is found only in Christ and with Christ. Failure to understand this truth is related to our next mental obstacle.

"I just want to be happy."

Our world bombards us with the message that we deserve to be happy and that personal fulfillment is our highest goal. When we do not feel happy, we must do whatever it takes to make ourselves feel better. This may include discarding people or things in our life that contribute to our present unhappiness or that might hinder our future satisfaction.

Pursuing a gratifying life is a reasonable goal. It seems unnatural and crazy to deliberately choose a path that appears to sacrifice personal happiness. Many people, even some well-meaning Christians, would advise David or Darlene to give up and divorce their unresponsive spouse. They might counsel, "You've tried long enough. You deserve to be happy." The dilemma comes as we struggle to decide which path brings true happiness: the world's path or God's path?

Jesus is even more concerned with our personal happiness than the world is. His way of attaining it, however, is diametrically opposed to the world's way. He tells us, "Blessed [happy] are those who hunger and thirst for righteousness, for they will be filled" (Matthew 5:6). Jesus teaches us that happiness isn't found by pursuing the things we think will make us happy, such as a perfect marital relationship. Instead, he tells us, real happiness is found when we pursue *him* and his righteousness (a right relationship with him).

Even Christians often believe that the purpose of marriage is to fulfill us and make us happy. However, Jesus tells us that only *he* will fulfill us and make us happy. When the psalmist tells us to "Delight yourself in the LORD and he will give you the desires of your heart" (Psalm 37:4), he doesn't mean we have to grit our teeth and obey God in order to get the things we really want. He is saying delight (take pleasure or enjoyment) in God and his ways. (See, for example, Psalm 1:2; Psalm 35:9-10; Psalm 43:4; Psalm 112:1; Isaiah 61:10.) It is easy to profess delight in God while really believing the opposite—that seeking the heart of God is boring, usually difficult, and full of hardship. Yet Jesus tells us that his principles are not dry crusts of tasteless bread that we must force-feed ourselves for survival; they are the very bread of life, nourishing to the depths of our soul. When the psalmist encourages us to "taste and see that the LORD is good" (Psalm 34:8), how many of us think that is just nice poetry rather than truth? Generally, only in the hardships of life do we forage for the deeper spiritual food. In easier times, we are content with snacks.

God's Word also warns us of another path that leads to hardship. He tells us "the rebellious live in a sun-scorched land" (Psalm 68:6) and "the way of the unfaithful is hard" (Proverbs 13:15). Too often we disregard his warning, believing instead the lies of the world and Satan that tempt us to doubt God's Word and ways. We strike out on our own paths of personal happiness and self-fulfillment. Part of maturity involves learning to *trust* that God knows what he is doing and that personal hardship will be used to mold us into the image of Christ, which he says is very, very good (Romans 8:28-29). It is not wrong or selfish to seek our own happiness, but we are misguided and deceived to think that any real or lasting happiness can be found apart from knowing, loving, and obeying God. (See Jeremiah 2:11-13 and 1 Peter 1:8.)

"I don't feel like it."

I was encouraging Sandra to apply some of these principles to her own marriage when she said, "I just don't feel like it, and I don't want to be a hypocrite." Many of us, like Sandra, are under the impression "that if we don't *feel* something there can be no authenticity in *doing* it. But the wisdom of God says something different, namely, that we can *act* ourselves into a new way of feeling much quicker than we can *feel* ourselves into a new way of acting."[5] Choosing to act right when you don't feel like it isn't hypocrisy; it's obedience. Making this choice, however, involves more than mere behavioral change. Obedience does not mean we learn to smile with love on the outside while screaming with hate on the inside. Our heart and our mind must be engaged as well, even if our emotions are reluctant. Jesus yielded to God in the Garden of Gethsemane. He didn't yield because he felt like it but because he wanted to please God. He believed God's plan was true and right. Jesus didn't just grit his teeth and say, "Okay, if I have to." Yielding is a conscious choice to submit ourselves to God's plan, not just with our body, but also with our mind, emotions, and will. We give our entire heart to God. We choose to trust him, even when our feelings aren't necessarily eager to do so.

"I am afraid to trust God completely."

Many of us claim to trust God, but when it comes to really having to do it, we run scared. I, too, used to be afraid of yielding to God, of trusting him totally with my life. I was afraid he would make me go to

Africa, make me give up my blow dryer, and make me eat bugs. Many of us are deceived by Satan into believing that if we really trust God, our lives will be miserable, full of hardship and suffering. The French theologian François Fénelon encourages us in this by asking us: "What are you afraid of? Of following too much goodness, finding a too-loving God; of being drawn by an attraction which is stronger than self or the charms of this poor world? What are you afraid of? Of becoming too humble, too detached, too pure, too true, too reasonable, too grateful to your Father which is in heaven?" He goes on: "I pray you, be afraid of nothing so much as of this false fear—this foolish, worldly wisdom which hesitates between God and self, between vice and virtue, between gratitude and ingratitude, between life and death."[6]

Sometimes we are afraid to trust God because we believe that what *we* want will bring us delight and happiness. We fear that if we trust God he will ask us to sacrifice our desires. The apostle Paul tells us that there is nothing greater than knowing God and that God will never ask us to sacrifice this. Paul experienced many earthly honors and great achievements. Yet none of them were worth anything to him compared to knowing God (Philippians 3:4-11). If we want to become more like our Lord, we will need to learn to sacrifice at times within the context of our marriage. *Sacrifice my time? my dreams? my desires? my felt needs?* Yes, God may call you to lay those things down at times in order to learn to love. We know this is part of the process of our maturity, but we actually *learn* to do it by practicing it within the everyday duties and responsibilities of our marital and family relationships.

My friend has a personal trainer who makes her do the craziest things to whip her into shape. One day he took the seat off her stationary bicycle and made her pedal while standing up. She thought he was nuts and initially resisted his instructions. But he assured her that this indeed was good for her. It would strengthen her legs and burn more calories than if she rested her bottom on the seat. Sure enough, it worked, and she was delighted with the results.

Sometimes God puts us through difficult training, and we struggle against it. Yet if we can begin to see what God is up to during our marital difficulties, we will begin to get a glimpse of his master plan, which is for our absolute good and happiness. James 1 tells us that the trials and troubles we experience develop in us a character trait known as perseverance. When we understand perseverance, we will be well on our way toward maturity. The apostle Paul also affirmed this truth, reminding us that perseverance and faith are developed through our trials in life and that in such circumstances our faith grows stronger and deeper (Romans 5:3-5). Just as stronger muscles are built through strenuous exercise, these internal character qualities are built into us through our difficulties—unless we bail out of the process and try to take a shortcut to happiness and maturity.

Just as my friend eventually had to decide to believe and trust her trainer so she could gain maximum benefit from her exercise routine (after all, that was what she was paying him for), we must choose whether we will believe God and trust him so that we will remain steadfast when we are panting and sweating, tempted to give up.

Loving God, Loving Others

There's more to acting right when our spouse acts wrong than just developing more Christlike outward actions. Becoming more and more like Jesus means learning to exercise in our heart and our home the two greatest commandments Jesus gave us—to love the Lord God with all our heart, soul, mind, and strength, and to love our neighbor as ourselves (Mark 12:30-31). Our closest neighbor is our spouse. Jesus didn't intend for us to live out these commandments intellectually, but personally and practically. Jesus had a lot to say about the Pharisees, who acted right on the outside while their hearts were unresponsive and cold on the inside (Matthew 15:8). Just *acting* right doesn't please God when our heart isn't engaged in the process.

Throughout this book I will challenge you to grow in your relationship with God so that you will love him with all your heart, soul, mind, and strength. Throughout the Gospels, Jesus always zeros in on what is in our heart. He asks us what we love and what we worship. He wants us to love him first with everything that is in us and then to love others (especially our spouse) as much as we love ourselves. As we embark on this process, we will discover that we have other loves. We will have to choose which comes first. Do we love Jesus, or do we love happiness, self-fulfillment, and our own way? Jesus tells us, "Where your treasure is, there your heart will be also" (Matthew 6:21). Our marriage, like no other relationship, reveals what we love. Our marriage exposes us, and we can't hide or fake it for very long. The real us, with all our strengths and weaknesses, tumbles out. What we love and what we worship will be expressed in our marriage, especially when we do not get what we want or think we need. Chapter 2 will help us to understand how God uses our spouse's wrongs to expose us—much like a mirror—and reveal what is going on in our heart. This is necessary as the first step in our growth, for we cannot change what we do not see.

Dear Jesus,

I confess that I am afraid to let go completely. I am afraid to trust you fully for my happiness and well-being. I do want a good marriage. I want to get along with my spouse and have a home that is full of laughter and caring, respect and love. But even more than that, Lord, I am beginning to see that you may use the present difficulties in my marriage to teach me to be more like you. Help me be a willing student in the school of holiness. Thank you for all the things that my spouse does that irritate, hurt, or trouble me, for this is the very sandpaper you will use to rub off my rough edges. Help me to submit to your refining process with a willing and yielded heart. Teach me your ways: how to love unselfishly, how to forgive when I don't want to, how to speak the truth in love when I need to, and how to overcome evil with good. Those characteristics are so foreign to me. Remind me what life and marriage are all about, Lord. Loving you, serving you, glorifying you, and reflecting you to others, especially those I live with, will bring me my greatest joy. Dear Jesus, make me more willing and increase my faith. For I desire to love you with all my heart, soul, strength, and will.

Amen.

TWO

WHAT DO MY SPOUSE'S WRONGS REVEAL IN ME?

The quickest way to the heart is through a wound.

JOHN PIPER

It's been said, "Adversity introduces a man to himself." Before I got married, I pictured myself as a giving and easygoing person. Once married, I began to get a glimpse of another side of *me,* one that I neither was aware existed nor found attractive. I saw how much I liked my own way and how angry I could get when I didn't get it. I also got a peek at the huge amount of pride I had when I believed I was right and my husband did not. I saw how I had a tendency to hang on to my hurts (even nurse them along) and how little I was willing to forgive and let go of things my husband did that I didn't like or approve of. Before I got married, I could end a relationship if I got hurt or upset. But as a Christian, I knew I would need to stay in my marriage and work it out, even apologize! These were lessons that I did not like to learn, nor did I find them easy. When I got married at the ripe old age of twenty-three, I loved being loved, and I loved being *in* love—that was the easy part. But I didn't have a clue about how to love unconditionally or sacrificially. God has had to teach me about real love, often using as practice sessions those very times that Howard wasn't acting the way I wanted him to.

Often when counseling married couples, I see the same patterns emerge. One question I ask is "When did your problems start?" Often the answer is "I didn't realize I had problems until I got married." God sanctifies us, purifies us, and teaches us *how* to become more like him in the context of our relationships. How can we learn to love or to live selflessly *alone?* We can't. For those of us who are married, our most intimate adult relationship is our marriage. In it, much of our emotional and spiritual maturity will take place—but only if we allow God and others to teach us.

Instead of looking at what our spouse is doing that is upsetting, hurtful, or wrong *to* us, we must begin by redirecting our attention toward what our spouse's wrongs reveal *in* us. God may be using his or her imperfections, differences, weaknesses, and sins to teach us valuable lessons on how to forgive, how to forbear, how to have self-control, how to speak the truth in love, and how to love our enemies. Jeanne Guyon compares this exposing process to a tree being stripped of its leaves in preparation for winter. She says: "The tree is no longer beautiful in its surface appearance. But has the tree actually changed? Not at all. Everything is *exactly* as it was before. Everything is as it has *always* been! It is just that the leaves are no longer there to *hide* what is *real*. The beauty of the outward life of the leaves had only hidden what had always been present." She goes on to say: "We can each look so beautiful...until life disappears! Then, no matter who, the Christian is

revealed as full of defects. As the Lord works on you to produce purifi-
cation, you will appear stripped of all your virtues! But, in the tree,
there *is* life inside; and, as the tree, you are not actually becoming
worse, you are simply seeing yourself for what you really are!"[1]

Whenever our spouse does something we don't like, we have a
response. Our feelings are aroused. Our mind races, and we usually act
out what our thoughts and feelings are telling us.

This happens so fast that we often describe it as a knee-jerk reaction. We don't stop to think about how we want to respond or what
would in fact be the best response. We just react. Although some might
believe that the wounds we experience *make* us react a certain way, that
thinking is not accurate. For example, when I am waiting in a long line
with a slow clerk, I feel impatient and irritated. The clerk is not *making*
me feel impatient and angry. She is just the trigger that reveals the
impatience and anger that is already in my heart. When someone does
something that displeases us or hurts us, that person doesn't *cause* our
feelings, but our reaction to the situation reveals something about who
we are. Jesus reinforced this notion when he said, "The good man
brings good things out of the good stored up in his heart, and the evil
man brings evil things out of the evil stored up in his heart. *For out of
the overflow of his heart his mouth speaks*" (Luke 6:45). We can all look
good on the outside (when we have all our leaves on our branches), but
our reaction to life's difficulties, specifically our marital difficulties, strip
us and give us a glimpse of what is really going on in our heart.

Learning to look at ourselves instead of at our spouse in these situations allows us to take the plank out of our own eye before attempting
to remove the speck in our spouse's eye (Matthew 7:5). It also keeps us
from being the judge of our mate's motives and actions. It reminds us

of our own failures and weaknesses, and this enables us to speak to our spouse with humility because we are mindful that we, too, have a long way to go.

For most of us, love comes easily when our spouse is doing what we want. But when that doesn't happen, the contents of our heart's darker side come spilling out. Then love becomes much harder. In his book *Sacred Marriage,* Gary Thomas wrote, "If you want to become more like Jesus, I can't imagine any better thing to do than to get married. Being married forces you to face some character issues you'd never have to face otherwise."[2]

In our homes we can allow the anvil of difficult circumstances to forge us into a better image of Christ, or we can become beaten down in discouragement, flattened by repeated conflict, and hardened by bitterness, eventually becoming cold and colorless, going through the motions of marriage and Christianity but having no heart for it.

A line from one of my favorite songs says, "Purify my heart, let it be as gold and precious silver." Sounds wonderful, but how does this happen? Gold is refined by constant heating in a fiery furnace, where all its impurities rise to the surface. When they are scraped off, only beautiful, pure gold remains. God purifies our heart in the fire of hardship and adversity. Often we are not even aware of the impurities in our heart until we are put in the fire of a difficult marriage and the dross rises to the surface. During this time, I believe God's intention for you is to examine your own responses to your spouse's wrongdoing. God may use the very actions of your spouse that you find so annoying or troubling to reveal the contents of your heart to you so that *you* can grow and change. That is part of the purifying and refining process.

As we begin to take a look at what our spouse's wrongs reveal in us, a jumble of emotions, thoughts, expectations, and personal sins is likely to surface. Honesty about this is necessary for those of us who want to clearly see what or who we rely on for our happiness, security, and well-being. Is it God? Or is our welfare more dependent upon getting what we want?

Our Spouse's Wrongs Reveal the Negative or Inaccurate Way We Interpret Life

Tom came home from work eager to share with Sonia the good news about his job promotion. But as soon as he walked through the door, Sonia plunked the baby in his arms and informed him she'd had it. She needed some time to herself and dashed off to the mall. Tom felt hurt and dejected. As he stewed he began thinking, *Sonia doesn't care about me. She never asks me how my day is. She just wants to unload hers. She doesn't appreciate how hard I work.* The more Tom stewed, the more angry and hurt he felt. When Sonia came home she felt much better and was eager to talk with Tom, but Tom ignored her. She sat next to him, but he got up and went to bed. Then Sonia felt hurt and rejected. She thought, *What's with him? Doesn't he realize how hard I work, how difficult it can be to stay home all day with a cranky baby? He resents having to take care of our child. Why should I have to beg him to take her off my hands? I need a break too.*

When both Sonia and Tom behaved in ways the other didn't like, they each reacted with negative interpretations. In situations like this, it is tempting to focus all our attention on how our spouse has hurt or angered us. It is crucial, however, that we begin to understand that our feelings are caused not by our spouse's behavior, but by the way we interpret his or her behavior.

When our spouse does something we don't like, we usually have a negative response. This response is always a mixture of our thoughts and feelings, which often leads to less than Christlike behavior. Let's start with Tom. When Sonia left, Tom interpreted Sonia's behavior in a certain subjective way. He told himself she didn't care; she didn't think of him or his needs. But were those thoughts true or accurate?

Like Tom, we believe that our feelings are *caused* by the situation. But let's look at this misconception more closely. Could Tom have thought about what Sonia did in a different light? Tom's feelings of hurt and anger were caused by his interpretation of Sonia's actions, not by Sonia's actions. (See Chart 1.)

Situation or Marital Trouble	Tom's Thoughts	Feelings	Behavior
Sonia left for the mall.	She doesn't care about me.	hurt	sulking
	She never asks me how my day is.	anger	stewing
	She just wants to unload hers.	anger	withdrawal
	She doesn't appreciate how hard I work.	hurt	withdrawal

CHART 1

We can readily see that Tom's *thoughts* about Sonia's behavior had more to do with his emotional response and subsequent withdrawal than Sonia's *actual* behavior. But we must ask a larger question: Why did Tom interpret Sonia's behavior in this negative way? As sinful human beings, we all have a heart that is oriented around self-serving interests. If Tom had thought more in the moment about Sonia's needs than his own, he may have interpreted her behavior differently. For instance, he could have thought, *Wow, she must have really had a bad day. She usually doesn't act this way. I need to be supportive. I can tell her about the good news later after giving her some relief.* Tom could have remained calm throughout the evening, enjoyed precious time with his daughter, and shared his good news as soon as Sonia returned home.

Now let's turn to Sonia's thoughts. When Tom went to bed early without talking with her, she, too, interpreted his behavior in a negative way. She knew Tom was angry, but she thought he was angry because he resented taking care of the baby. Although this might be a reasonable interpretation, we know it is not true. Again, her interpretation of why Tom acted the way he did had more to do with her feelings than with Tom's actual behavior. (See Chart 2.)

Marital Trouble	Sonia's Thoughts	Feelings	Behavior
Tom went to bed.	He doesn't realize how hard I work and how difficult it can be to stay home all day with a cranky baby.	rejection	sulked
	He resents having to take care of our child.	disappointment	cried
	Why should I have to beg him to take her off my hands? I need a break too.	resentment	withdrew; ignored Tom the next day

CHART 2

The first step in learning to act right when our spouse acts wrong is to examine our own thoughts in specific situations. Each of us forms an interpretive lens through which we view our external circumstances or what is happening around us. Again, our interpretations about a situation, not the situation itself, cause in large part our emotional reactions to it.

Once while my husband and I were teaching a Sunday-school class on marriage, a woman confided in me that she was having marital problems. She wasn't sure she wanted to stay married anymore. When I asked her what was wrong she said, "My husband's too nice." As shocking as this sounds, this particular woman interpreted her husband's kindness in a negative way—so much so that it made her increasingly frustrated and unhappy. What was this woman telling herself about her husband's niceness that made it feel bad to her?

When Jesus performed miracles, some people hailed him as the Son of God. Others saw him as a sham, and still others believed he was from the devil (John 10). Their *interpretation* of Jesus' behavior, *not Jesus' behavior,* determined their response to him. Those who thought he was a sham walked away. Those who believed he was from Satan wanted to kill him. Those who worshiped him believed he performed miracles because he was from God. Each of these actions is a response to the same behavior; the interpretation of the behavior is what made the difference.

We interpret all our spouse's behaviors, labeling each as good or bad, kind or mean, wrong or right. Sometimes our interpretations are inaccurate. Part of understanding ourselves and growing through our marriage difficulties is to recognize that we interpret all behavior through a lens that colors our understanding of things and to recognize that our lens may not always be telling us the truth.

Whenever I read through the Old Testament, I am particularly struck by this phenomenon. For example, in Deuteronomy 9 we read that the Israelites had subdued nations stronger than they were. God told them not to interpret their victory incorrectly. He said, "Do not say to yourself, 'The LORD has brought me here to take possession of this land *because of my righteousness.*'" He warned, "No, it is on account of the wickedness of these nations that the LORD is going to drive them out." God understands that the way we think about something or interpret a situation will in large part determine how we feel about it. God warned the Israelites against interpreting their victory incorrectly to prevent them from becoming proud and self-confident.

Research has shown that one of the greatest threats to a marriage occurs when spouses regularly interpret each other's behaviors negatively.[3] When this happens, just like the woman from my Sunday-school class, even good behaviors like kindness are cast in a negative light. When our spouse acts wrong (from our perspective), we need to stop and check out our thinking. Consider what you are telling yourself about your spouse's behavior, and question if there is another way to look at it. Scripture's "love chapter" (1 Corinthians 13) tells us that love believes all things.

Begin to give your spouse the benefit of the doubt until you've had a chance to talk with him or her about whatever is troubling you. You may find yourself overly upset for nothing. Certainly Tom might have been disappointed when Sonia ran out of the house before he had a chance to share his good news. However, had he not indulged in the negative and untrue thoughts that followed, by the time Sonia returned he may have worked through his disappointment and been able to talk calmly with her. Had Sonia talked with Tom, she might have been spared the anger and disappointment she felt when she believed Tom's anger was evidence of resentment toward their child.

At times our spouse's actions *are* hurtful, unkind, or sinful. We aren't thinking negatively; we've interpreted things truthfully. Yet in learning to act right when our spouse acts wrong, self-examination remains an important first step. Thomas à Kempis said, "Occasions of adversity discover best how great virtue each one has. For such occasions do not make a man frail, but they reveal what sort he is."[4] Throughout this book I will talk about how to respond correctly when our spouse sins against us. First, however, let's make sure our interpretations of our spouse's behavior aren't the result of an overactive imagination or negative thinking patterns that flow from a self-centered heart.

Our Spouse's Wrongs Expose Baggage from Our Past

Stacey was beside herself with fear and jealousy. She became furious whenever her husband had friendly conversations with other women. Each time Stan watched television, Stacey scrutinized how long Stan's eyes would linger on the actresses. Stacey believed her husband was acting wrong. She wanted him to stop talking with other women and tried monitoring his TV habits, which drove him crazy. Stacey repeatedly accused Stan of immoral thoughts and was convinced he secretly wished he had married someone else.

Stan denied Stacey's accusations and tried to reassure her. "I'm just being a normal guy living in a normal world. Stacey goes ballistic if I even say hello to an old friend at church." If we look at some of Stacey's thinking, we can easily see what was making her so upset. (See Chart 3.)

Situation	Stacey's Thoughts	Feelings	Behaviors
Stan's TV viewing	He looks at pretty women.	jealousy	judging
	He wishes he could be with them.	disgust, betrayal	accusing
Stan's friendliness to other women	He would rather be with them.	hurt, rejection	crying
	He is just like all men.	fury	badgering
	I can't trust him.	fear	controlling

CHART 3

Over time Stacey began to realize that her thoughts about her husband's behavior were irrational and untrue, but she felt powerless to stop them. Stacey was beside herself and couldn't convince herself otherwise, despite reassurances by Stan. What was going on? Why did Stacey interpret Stan's actions in such a negative way?

When Stacey was a child, her father engaged in multiple extramarital affairs. Stacey's mother warned her, "Men can't be trusted; they are only out for one thing." Stacey's tendency over the years to choose men likely to fulfill this belief simply reinforced it. After Stacey became a Christian, she sought a man who would be different. Stan was that man, or so she thought. He had been raised in a Christian home, had good moral values, and had treated her respectfully before they got married. She thought her worries about men were over—until she saw Stan act friendly with other women. Stacey concluded that Christian men were no different from others. *Therefore, Stan cannot be trusted; he is out for only one thing.*

Our beliefs, whether they be religious or otherwise, form the interpretive lens through which we view all incoming information. This lens colors the data in a way that reinforces our beliefs, and it forms the foundation for why we tend to think a particular way about a situation. For example, Stacey's internal beliefs told her not to trust men. When Stan spoke to other women or watched television programs that featured attractive women, Stacey had certain thoughts about Stan's behaviors. But her thoughts were not random. Stacey interpreted Stan's actions in a particular way because of her internal beliefs, which influenced the way she thought about Stan's behaviors.

Stacey's thoughts *(Stan is attracted to other women; he wishes he hadn't married me; he is only interested in sex, just like every other man I've known)* led her to feelings of jealousy, hurt, and anger. These feelings affected how she acted. She pouted, withdrew, and accused Stan of having or wanting an affair. Her irrational behavior caused Stan to withdraw from Stacey, which then reinforced Stacey's belief that she was right! *Stan doesn't want to be with me. Men can't be trusted!* (See Diagram 1.)

In Scripture, Job's friends are a good example of how one's beliefs influence an interpretation of events. Job's friends believed bad things happen to bad people and good things happen to good people. When Job's calamities occurred, Job's friends sincerely tried to help. They reasoned if bad things were happening in Job's life, Job must have done something wrong to deserve them. Despite Job's protests to the contrary, his friends interpreted all of Job's troubles through this exclusive lens. Jesus later challenged the belief that bad things happen to bad people and corrected it with truth so people would not always view calamities as punishment from God. (See Luke 13.)

Diagram 1

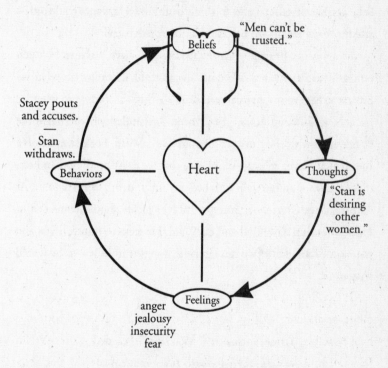

Trigger:
—
**Stan is watching TV or talking to
an attractive female friend.**

Beliefs

"Men can't be
trusted."

Stacey pouts
and accuses.
—
Stan
withdraws.

Behaviors

Heart

Thoughts

"Stan is
desiring
other
women."

anger
jealousy
insecurity
fear

Feelings

When our spouse's behavior triggers certain thoughts in us, it's worth our time to examine whether those thoughts are true. Consider also whether our thoughts tend to fall into a repetitive pattern. Like Stacey, we might discover some deeply held internal beliefs that influence the way we interpret a situation. If those beliefs are not embedded in truth, we must work to uproot them from our heart so they will no longer influence the way we interpret our circumstances. Paul tells us we are transformed by the renewing of our mind (Romans 12:2). Our heavenly Father designed our brains so that our thoughts and feelings are related. He knows that our deepest beliefs, true or not, will shape the way we view life. God wants to transform our heart so that we will believe what he tells us and to think truthfully. He wants his Word— and his Word alone—to become our interpretive lens.

Many of us struggle with this because we have a chasm between our head and our heart. We don't always think according to what we profess to believe as Christians; instead, we think according to what we *really* believe—deep down in our heart—regardless of whether those beliefs align with the truth set forth in God's Word. For example, on a rudimentary level, all humans believe that we don't need God and can make life work on our own (this belief is our prideful, sinful nature). As Christians, of course, our interpretive lens of life should come out of our relationship with God and his Word. He seeks to transform us and renew our thoughts so we can interpret things truthfully—as he would have us to.

Our Spouse's "Wrongs" Reveal Our Unrealistic Expectations

Most of us enter marriage with some pretty unrealistic expectations of what the relationship will be like. Some of us get our expectations from Hollywood: Love is little more than fun, passion, and romance. Others of us have longed for the more spiritual side of marriage and have read books about strong Christian husbands and wives who have devotions together, pray together, and talk intimately for an hour a day. Men often long for a wife who is a combination of June Cleaver and a Victoria's Secret model. Women secretly desire a mixture of Harrison Ford, James Dobson, and Mr. Fix-It. We feel keenly disappointed when our spouse falls short of our ideals. "It doesn't take long for the newlyweds to discover that 'everything in one person nobody's got.'"[5]

Sometimes we try to remake our spouse into our ideal mate. When he or she resists (which is always), we are disappointed and may accuse them of not doing something that they *should* be doing or are *supposed* to be doing. John was disappointed when Donna wouldn't wear the sexy clothes he bought her. She told him they weren't her style and she felt uncomfortable wearing them. They were too tight and too low cut. John accused her of being unsubmissive and unloving by refusing to wear things that made her look attractive to him. If John would step back for a moment and look at himself when he believed Donna was acting wrong, he might see that his expectations of his wife (that she totally remake herself into the image he desired) are unrealistic and unloving, not to mention self-centered. He married Donna looking the way she did; why was he now trying to remake her?

Our Spouse's Wrongs Reveal the Idols of Our Heart

Sheila came home from her women's retreat eager to share with her husband, Jeff, what wonderful things she had learned that weekend. But when she walked in the door, Sheila was assaulted by a pungent odor, and she found the kitchen piled high with dirty dishes. Toys were strewn everywhere, and dirty laundry still lay in front of the washer. Jeff was sleeping on the couch with the television blaring. The baby was in her playpen with a dirty diaper. Instantly Sheila lost all her enthusiasm and spiritual resolve. She lit into Jeff. "Why couldn't you pick up before I got home? You just left everything for me to do *as always!* I can't go away for a couple of days without coming home to a mess. What's wrong with you?"

Sheila was furious. It wasn't because she was thinking untrue thoughts. Her husband *had* let her down, and this wasn't the first time. He regularly disappointed her when she asked him to do something. He left projects either undone or only partially complete. Sheila longed for a husband who would be helpful and responsible, and time after time Jeff failed her. She wanted a partner who would willingly share in taking good care of their home and children. Talking with him previously about this hadn't produced any real change. Yelling made things worse; Jeff just withdrew even more. Sheila felt hopeless. She was angry with Jeff and now was angry with herself for blowing up, especially since she had just felt so close to the Lord during her weekend retreat.

It's important to recognize the desires of our heart because they deeply influence our thoughts and actions. Our desires have been called "the atomic energy of our soul." They give us energy, direction, and focus. Sheila wanted her husband to be more responsible and helpful. Her desires for these things are legitimate and normal; they are desires most spouses have. Sheila is not wrong for having them. But consider what happened *to* Sheila and *in* Sheila when she didn't get what she desired. What came up and out of her heart when Jeff failed her *again?* In her legitimate disappointment and anger, Sheila lost control of her tongue and her temper. Although her husband was clearly wrong, how can Sheila learn to act right in these circumstances? What might God be trying to show Sheila that will help her become more like him? Oswald Chambers tells us that "we compromise with evil whenever we try to satisfy our desires at the expense of doing the will of God."[6]

Sheila's desires were not sinful, but her reaction to Jeff's failure revealed that her desires *were* out of order. God wants the preeminent desire of our heart to be to know him and to be like him. John Calvin said that the evil in our desires typically does not lie in what we want, but that we want it too much.[7] The apostle Paul expressed this clearly in Philippians 3:8-10, where he wrote that he counted everything to be rubbish compared to knowing Christ. The deepest desire of Paul's heart was to know Jesus and to be conformed to his image. When our other desires, however good and legitimate, take first place in our heart, God calls them idols. We will be controlled by them instead of by God. God often allows life's circumstances to reveal our primary desires or first loves, so that we can see that they have become idols. They are those things (apart from God) we think we need for life, happiness, and well-being. God revealed to Sheila that she was basing her well-being upon the actions of her husband. God wanted Sheila's well-being to be dependent upon him.

Let's look at how Jesus responded when his desires were frustrated. What did Jesus do when he didn't get what he wanted? In the Garden of Gethsemane, Jesus asked his disciples to pray for him during the hardest trial of his earthly life. Jesus desired his friends' support. They failed him. They repeatedly fell asleep. Yet Jesus handled his disappointment in the right way because his *primary* desire was to obey and please God in all things. The right way doesn't mean pretending it didn't happen *or* it didn't hurt. He was honest and spoke to the disciples about his disappointment, but he also forgave them (Mark 14:32–41). His well-being was centered in God, not in the fulfillment of his desires.

Our Spouse's Wrongs Reveal Our Fears and Insecurities

Bob noticed that his wife, Pamela, was at it again. She seemed to have an insatiable need to flirt with other men. She had already been involved in one extramarital affair; now it looked as if she was headed that way again. Yet Bob said nothing. In fact, after Pam confessed her first affair, he quickly let it drop and never mentioned it again. Bob and Pam never examined why Pam had the affair, never spoke of it, never went to counseling. What prevented Bob from daring to look at the root of this marital problem? What were Pam's sinful behaviors exposing in Bob's heart?

Bob was afraid. He was terrified that Pam would eventually leave him for another man. As a child, he had always felt shy and inadequate. Becoming a Christian had done little to change his inner feelings of self-doubt and inferiority. He was thrilled that a beautiful woman like Pam would want to marry him. Now he was afraid of losing her—so afraid that he could not set appropriate boundaries in their marriage, share his feelings with Pam, or speak the truth in love to her (although she had invited him to confront her when he noticed her acting inappropriately toward other men). God wanted Bob to grow out of his passivity and learn to handle his fears so that he could function as a true helpmate to Pam.

God didn't *cause* Pam to act wrong, but he could *use* Pam's wrong actions to promote Bob's growth if Bob would examine what Pam's behaviors revealed in him. Bob would need to face the fears and insecurities that prevented him from setting appropriate boundaries with Pam. She needed his help and had invited him to give it, yet his fears prevented him from offering the very thing she desperately needed.

Our Spouse's Wrongs Expose Our Sins

As I mentioned at the beginning of this chapter, getting married revealed many shortcomings in my heart that I never knew existed. Certain sins are only revealed through our interactions with others. When we are alone, they remain hidden and obscure. Often when we *think* our spouse is acting wrong, these very sins—particularly pride and selfishness—are in fact being displayed in us. Of course, our sins aren't exposed only when our spouse acts wrong, but also during more neutral interactions within the marital relationship as well.

About forty rosebushes grace a gentle slope along my driveway. A noxious weed grows among these beautiful blooms. It disguises itself as a flower, but the plant is lethal to my roses. Left unchecked, it gradually wraps itself around the rose stalks and slowly kills the plant. I've tried ripping these weeds out, but they have a massive underground root system. To kill the weed I would have to kill the roses. The best I can do is regularly watch for them and, when I see them, yank them out. Like the weed among the roses, pride and selfishness are rooted deep within our heart. We must ask the Holy Spirit to keep watch over us and to help us yank them out when we see them. Left unchecked, they can damage our life and our home.

Pride

Pride is a slippery sin. Sometimes it is hard to get our hands around it. We can see results of pride in others but are often blind to it in our own lives. The psalmist declares, "For in his own eyes he flatters himself too much to detect or hate his sin" (Psalm 36:2). Pride robs us of growth. It chokes out fruitfulness and lies to us about what ultimately matters. Oswald Chambers simply states, "Pride is the deification of self."[8] When we make ourselves God, we are always right, always first, always in control, and always the most important. We want everything to revolve around us and to be for us. Perhaps God is using our spouse to shatter this illusion for our own good, for pride is a deceiver (Jeremiah 49:16). Beth Moore writes a poem that exposes pride for what it is:

> My name is Pride. I am a cheater.
> I cheat you of your God-given destiny…because
> you demand your own way.
> I cheat you of contentment…because you
> "deserve better than this."
> I cheat you of knowledge…because you already
> know it all.
> I cheat you of healing…because you're too full of
> me to forgive.
> I cheat you of holiness…because you refuse to
> admit when you're wrong.
> I cheat you of vision…because you'd rather look
> in the mirror than out a window.
> I cheat you of genuine friendship…because
> nobody's going to know the real you.

I cheat you of love…because real romance
demands sacrifice.
I cheat you of greatness in heaven…because you
refuse to wash another's feet on earth.
I cheat you of God's glory…because I convince
you to seek your own.
My name is Pride. I am a cheater.
You like me because you think I'm always looking
out for you. Untrue.
I'm looking to make a fool of you.
God has so much for you, I admit, but don't worry…
If you stick with me
You'll never know.[9]

Often we think of pride as stubborn arrogance, but at other times our pride is revealed through our self-pitying withdrawal. Our pride is wounded and we retreat instead of repent. We are ashamed or feel guilty. Instead of turning to God and our spouse for forgiveness, we turn inward, nursing our wounded ego until the sting of our sin begins to dissipate and we can go on. Sadly, nothing changes, either in our own lives or in our marital relationship.

Selfishness

Pride and selfishness usually go together. It is hard to imagine one without the other. Our culture reinforces selfishness in marriage by constantly bombarding us with the message, "You deserve to be happy." Yet selfishness can be even more subtle and difficult to identify than pride. Selfishness can occur when I refuse to let you know me and I retreat into a self-protective mode. It can also occur when I pour myself sacrificially into my work or the lives of my children when I am hurt or disappointed with my spouse. Instead of investing in my marriage where I'm not seeing any return, I invest where I get some satisfaction and reward. "One of the most deeply ingrained forms of selfishness in human nature is that of misery. The isolation of misery is far more proud than any other form of conceit."[10]

David (from chapter 1) wanted to grow and be a better husband to Julie. God knew best what David needed in order for that growth to occur. Julie's wrongdoing exposed David's selfishness and his pride. As David began to see what God was up to in the midst of his marital difficulties, he looked to himself instead of to Julie for change. This important step began the process whereby David could grow into the kind of man God wanted him to become.

God Uses Our Spouse's Wrongs for Our Growth

People bring out the best in us *and* the worst in us. Oswald Chambers tells us, "The test of a man's religious life and character is not what he does in the exceptional moments of life, but what he does in the ordinary times, when there is nothing tremendous or exciting on."[11] I would add that the test also comes when other people in our life sin against, hurt, or disappoint us. Then who we are and what we are made of is more apparent, not only to others but also to ourselves. This is the perfect time to yield to God's refining process so that we might not just endure our hardship but grow from and through it. John Calvin encourages us by reminding us "that they may not become too complacent or delighted in married life, he [God] makes them distressed by the short-coming of their partners."[12]

Dear Lord,

Thank you for the person I married. Help me to remember that you have placed him/her as a life partner not only to bless me, but also to refine me—to help me mature and become more like you. Thank you for what you can do in me through the difficulties, imperfections, and sins of my spouse. Help me to believe that you are working in my life for good through all the hurts and troubles of my marriage, and give me the faith to trust you in the midst of these difficulties.

Lord, I want right now to take my eyes off my spouse's wrongs and look and see what happens to me during these times. Reveal any sins or idolatrous desires. Show me my wrong thinking patterns or untrue thoughts. Lord, I desire to have you as my first love. Help me to trust and believe that you love me and are always good. Keep me from trusting myself or my own version of things that may lead me astray of your purposes for my life and my marriage. Help me take this first step so that I might learn to act right whenever my spouse acts in a way I don't like.

Amen.

THREE

STOP REACTING, START RESPONDING

There must be things that a man will not do,
before he decides about those things that he will do.

MENCIUS

Jennifer came to her weekly counseling session grinning from ear to ear. "I finally get it," she said. "When I don't react to Paul's stupid remarks with a sarcastic dig, God actually works in his heart. This morning he was complaining again about my job. Instead of defending myself or criticizing him, I just said, 'I know, honey. It must be hard for you to take care of the kids when you've already had a full day.' He walked away from me as usual, but then something very different happened. He came right back and gave me a big hug and kiss."

Jennifer had learned an important lesson. When she reacted to her husband's criticisms about her evening job with her usual sarcasm and defensiveness, things between them got worse. She just reacted out of habit, without forethought. Most of us are so caught up by what our spouse is doing wrong that we don't stop to think how to respond to it;

we just react. We often live in the moment without contemplating the long-term consequences of our behaviors. We do not intentionally set out to ruin our marriage or hurt our mate, but our reactions can be like a lit match tossed into gasoline. Proverbs tells us that "reckless words pierce like a sword" (Proverbs 12:18). Our sinful and destructive reactions to our spouse's wrongs can cause additional damage and hurt not only to our marriage but to our children, whose little eyes and ears are tuned in to the emotional climate in our home. As mentioned earlier, our children see and hear how we act as parents, as spouses, and as Christians when we are hurt, angry, disappointed, or frustrated. Our children will learn far more by what they see in us than by what we formally teach them—all the more reason for us to examine our own reactions. Let's continue to focus on ourselves right now as we consider how to stop reacting sinfully to our spouse's wrongdoing.

Psychologist John Gottman researches what makes or breaks marriages. He asks the question, "How can you prevent a marriage from going bad—or rescue one that already has?" After extensive studies, Gottman claims, "I am now able to predict whether a couple will stay happily together or lose their way. I can make this prediction after listening to the couple interact in our Love Lab for as little as five minutes!" How can he know? "What can make a marriage work is surprisingly simple," he says. "Happily married couples aren't smarter, richer, or more psychologically astute than others. But in their day-to-day lives, they have hit upon a dynamic that keeps their negative thoughts and feelings about each other (which all couples have) from overwhelming their positive ones."[1] Other research on marital unhappiness suggests that there are four negative reactions that will lead a couple toward divorce.[2] Perhaps not surprisingly, God's Word has something to say about each: escalating a fight (Proverbs 15:1), negative comments (Proverbs 29:11), invalidating comments (Proverbs 25:20; 1 Peter 2:17), and withdrawal and avoidance (Ephesians 4:25; Matthew 5:23-24).

When we develop a pattern of reacting negatively, whether just in our thoughts or also in our emotions and behaviors, we get our marriage into trouble. In order to reverse this pattern, we need to take full responsibility for how we react or respond to our spouse. No blaming. No excuses. Remember, what we do and how we act is *influenced* by others but not *caused* by others.

After being married for eighteen years, Sharon decided that she needed some professional help. She felt frustrated with her husband's passivity and his unwillingness to initiate more intimate conversation or take mutual responsibility for their social life. Sharon reacted to John's passivity with nagging. When that didn't work she tried yelling. John retreated even further. The more she thought about it, the more negativity she felt toward John. The more negativity she felt, the more she reacted. The more she reacted, the more John withdrew. The more John withdrew, the more negative she felt about him and their relationship. Do you see a pattern here? If all we do is react to our spouse whenever he or she does something we don't like, we will send ourselves and our marriage into a downward spiral. Like a caustic acid, this accelerating cycle leaves a marriage full of holes, out of which leak any positive elements.

Our human reaction to mistreatment, hurt, or betrayal can be very strong, especially when the pain is inflicted by our spouse. During such a time, some of us actually *want* to be destructive—to lash back or get revenge. A line from the movie *The First Wives Club* that drew uproarious applause from audiences was "Don't get even; get everything."

Some of us clapped furiously because we could relate to the emotions the film's characters experienced.

Because of this human desire to retaliate when wronged, it is important to purposely slow down and think about our responses to our spouse. If our habitual reactions fall into any of the categories below, we must break these habits. Why? So that we don't further damage our marriage. (See Proverbs 15:17; 17:1; 21:9.) Some may think this discussion doesn't apply because our spouse has already damaged our marriage beyond repair. However, all of us need to cease destructive reactions, not just because it is good for our marriage, but also because it is good for us. Proverbs 21:23 tells us, "He who guards his mouth and his tongue keeps himself from calamity." Another proverb warns that "he who guards his lips guards his life, but he who speaks rashly will come to ruin" (13:3). Peter instructs us, "Whoever would love life and see good days must keep his tongue from evil and his lips from deceitful speech" (1 Peter 3:10).

In addition to sinful verbal reactions, God tells us to put off certain behaviors that are not in keeping with our new life in Christ. (See Ephesians 4:29,31 and Colossians 3:8.) Unfortunately, many such behaviors are the very things that we do in reaction to our spouse's wrongs. It bears repeating: Putting off these behaviors and replacing them with Christlike behaviors benefits us and our marriage; it also pleases God. This is a win-win proposition. In stopping our wrong reactions, we learn which responses might help our spouse, help our marriage, and help us to grow to be more like Christ so that we may glorify God in the process.

In saying that we should not react destructively, I'm not suggesting we should ignore wrong behaviors or the pain that these wrongs inflict.

Instead, we choose not to react sinfully or recklessly, because such reactions are not in keeping with who we are as God's children. He wants to teach us *how* to respond appropriately with a heart *and* life that please him. With that in mind, let's look at what we must first stop doing in order to act right when our spouse acts wrong.

Stop Reckless Words

Our tongue is a powerful weapon of good and of evil. The Bible tells us that it can be used to do incredible good or intense harm, to bless and to curse. It can be used to bring healing (Proverbs 12:18), and it can be used to crush a spirit (Proverbs 15:4). It is often with our tongue that we first start the process of reacting in destructive ways. We use our tongue to curse, to criticize, to complain, and to show utter contempt for our spouse. Proverbs 29:11 says, "A fool gives full vent to his anger, but a wise man keeps himself under control." When our spouse does something wrong, we usually feel angry. Yet the apostle Paul cautions us that when we are angry, we are not to sin (Ephesians 4:26). Our words are not to be used to tear anyone down, but to build them up according to their needs (Ephesians 4:29). When our spouses act wrong, they may need us to speak the truth to them, not only about how we feel but about what they have done. The truth always must be about what God says is true, good and bad, wrong and right—according to his Word, not just our own opinion—and it must always be spoken in love (Ephesians 4:15).

Our gestures, tone of voice, and body language can also be vehicles for reckless reactions. Folding our arms, rolling our eyes, or asking a question in a tone dripping with contempt will immediately shut down any constructive communication. When practiced regularly between a couple, these reactions will erode all feelings of goodwill and happiness between them.

We all wrestle at times with controlling our tongue. When we feel something strongly, it can be downright painful not to blurt it right out. The psalmist struggled with this: "I will watch my ways and keep my tongue from sin; I will put a muzzle on my mouth as long as the wicked are in my presence" (Psalm 39:1). Yet in this very same psalm (verses 2 and 3) we see that keeping quiet when someone acts wrong is pretty tough. Perhaps the psalmist wanted to lash out, to tell off evildoers. Silence didn't bring the psalmist satisfaction, just more anguish. There is something within us that feels good when we let someone have it with our words. Keeping quiet hurts—it hurts us! We have often been told that we shouldn't keep our destructive or negative feelings inside. Yet as I cautioned in my book *The TRUTH Principle*, blurting out destructive emotions is a lot like vomiting. You might feel better to get it out, but vomit belongs in the toilet, not on your spouse. In order to act right when our spouse acts wrong, we will need to learn to control our tongue as well as our destructive, negative emotions. The exercise of writing letters to my spouse (the kind that I don't send, that I rip up when I'm done) often helps rid me of the more destructive emotions. It also offers me the opportunity to clarify my feelings and thoughts in preparation for when I am in the right frame of mind to articulate them.

We can glean two other lessons through the experience of the psalmist. First, in order to maintain his vow of silence, he continued to reflect on the bigger picture. (What is God up to in all of this?) Second, he took note of his own sinfulness. (What do my enemy's wrongs show me about *me?*) I am not recommending a vow of silence as an appropriate response to our spouse's wrongdoing. However, keeping quiet or still *until* we can decide how to respond is an important first step in learning how to act right.

At this point some of you might be thinking, *So far so good. I don't lash out. I just ignore him or her and walk away.* These more passive reactions may look better than blowing up, but when used as a regular way of dealing with marital problems, they can be just as injurious to a marriage as exploding with reckless words. One kills like a bomb, the other like a slow cancer. Both are equally deadly; one just takes a little longer than the other.

Stop Withdrawing or Pretending All Is Well

Sharon was upset because Dan seemed to make his career a higher priority than his family. He worked long into the evenings, spent time on the computer when he was at home, and on weekends often went to the office. Once she tried talking with him about it, but he reminded her that they needed the extra money right now and he was doing the best he could. She didn't buy it, and Sharon began to deeply resent his passion for his work and his lack of devotion to her and their children. She didn't nag or criticize. She didn't blow up or throw a fit, she just shut down and withdrew into a silent shell. Dan was too busy to notice at the time, but when he finally did, Sharon was well on her way into serious clinical depression. Please don't misunderstand me. I'm not excusing Dan's behavior or his insensitivity, but Sharon's reaction to it ultimately hurt her and her family.

One of my pastors recently said, "You can sweep broken glass under the carpet, but eventually it will work its way through the rug and cut your foot." One of the ways we react to things in our spouse that we don't like, or that our spouse is actually doing wrong, is to avoid it altogether. We pretend we don't see it or that it doesn't bother us when what we need to do is confront it (Ephesians 4:25).

Jim noticed that Annie had been buying a lot of new things for the house lately: new curtains for the living room, a new rug for the bedroom, clothes for the kids, even a new computer. They were struggling to pay their bills and were already incurring huge interest on their unpaid credit card balances. Still, Annie continued to buy new things every week. Jim's reaction was to pretend not to notice or to care. Avoiding the topic of Annie's spending problem was not helping their marriage; it was only making things worse. Jim could have reacted by blowing up, calling Annie names, and threatening to cut up the credit cards. Instead he reacted by shutting down, keeping quiet, and avoiding the problem. This more passive reaction was just as harmful. By avoiding the problem, Jim would not be helpful to Annie or to their marriage. Plus, Jim's increasing resentment added additional strain to their relationship.

In order to act right, Jim needed to stop pretending that all was well. His natural reaction to stress and conflict was to shut down and avoid it. In order to become more like Jesus in his marriage, he would need to learn to respond differently. He would need to learn how to speak to Annie about her spending problem for her own good and the good of their marriage.

Making the Change from Reacting to Responding

Donna and Hank had been married for two years when her world came crashing in. One day she found a receipt for a mysterious post office box. The receipt led to evidence of a dreadful reality: Her husband had been deceiving her. He was hiding thousands of dollars in debt that he had incurred while visiting massage parlors and pornographic Internet sites. Donna reacted! She yelled, she screamed, she threw all of Hank's clothes out on the front lawn. She called his parents. She called her parents. She was beside herself with anger and shame. "How could he!" she sobbed.

Hank committed a wrong that is among the most difficult for a spouse to respond to rightly. Dishonesty, betrayal, and infidelity breach our marital promises. They deeply wound and can fatally injure the very foundation of any marital relationship. What do we do? As Christians, how can we respond to this behavior biblically? Should we turn the other cheek and allow our spouse to get away with anything? Should we retaliate and fight back when we've been treated cruelly or unfairly?

Many believe that Christ's teaching to turn the other cheek and go the extra mile excludes fighting back. However, the apostle Paul said that in some circumstances he found it best to fight back. Instead of fists or ugly words, however, he used different kinds of weapons. He used the weapons of righteousness (2 Corinthians 6:7). We are in a war—a war of good versus evil, but we are not to fight this war as the world does (2 Corinthians 10:3-4). Romans 12 tells us *how* we are to win this war against evil. We are to overcome evil with good. *Overcome* is a fighting word. It is active, something we *must* do so that we will never be eternally injured by evil despite being wounded by it. Do we fight back when our spouse commits evil against us? The answer is yes! But first, to avoid confusion, let's briefly describe whom we are fighting and what we are fighting for.

Whom Are We Fighting?

Our real enemy is not our spouse, as much as it might feel that way. Our enemy is Satan and the evil he stands for. Jesus tells us that Satan is a liar and a destroyer (John 8:44). Martin Luther warned: "Hourly the devil seeks to destroy us all. No sooner are you baptized than the devil lies in wait for you. If possible, he would kill you in your mother's womb. He begrudges us every kernel of grain in the field, every fish, every morsel of bread, every cherry or apple, or any happy experience."[3] Satan wants to ruin your marriage and your life. Peter advises us: "Be self-controlled and alert. Your enemy the devil prowls around like a roaring lion looking for someone to devour" (1 Peter 5:8). Sometimes he uses our spouse to accomplish that purpose, making him or her *feel* like the enemy. That is Satan's plan. His tactics always involve sin, and so we often end up fighting each other instead of fighting our real enemy. When we react sinfully to our spouse's wrongs, Satan wins. He accomplishes his goal—to destroy our homes and our lives, not to mention our witness for Christ.

Enemies can do a lot of damage (Psalm 143:3). Satan would even like us to believe that God is our enemy. He wanted Eve to think that God was not interested in her best interests when he forbade her to eat of the fruit of the tree of knowledge (Genesis 3:4-5). At times the most godly approach to handling our marital difficulties will seem like foolishness. Satan tries to deceive us into thinking that God's way will ultimately rob us of something good—like happiness or security. His strategy is always to make a sinful reaction look good and a righteous response look foolish.

Sandy filed for divorce because of her husband's longstanding affair with a coworker. Part of the settlement involved disclosure of finances.

Over the thirty years they had been married, Sandy had put aside some money in savings bonds for their children's college education and other long-term retirement needs, even though her husband had plenty of savings and investments from his high-paying job. The kids were grown and college had been paid for, and she never paid much attention to the accumulation of this fund. When she inquired, she found she had acquired a substantial little nest egg.

During the divorce proceedings, Sandy learned that her husband had not been honest with her during their marriage regarding their financial affairs. She was tempted not to disclose her secret fund to the lawyers during settlement. Satan was tempting her to react sinfully to her husband's wrong. *It would be crazy to tell him of this extra money when he hid thousands of dollars from me in foreign bank accounts. He is a jerk; I'd be a fool to be honest and play by such an outdated principle.* What would Sandy do? Whom would she believe? Her husband was not her real enemy, although Satan certainly used him to hurt Sandy. Sandy would only make the right choice and overcome evil with good when she clearly identified her true enemy. Doing so gave her the ability to fight wisely, with the truth. She disclosed her nest egg. She may ultimately lose some of that money, but she has retained her integrity.

What Are We Fighting For?

It is equally crucial that we understand what we are fighting for. When my husband and I fight, I usually lose sight of this important detail. I end up fighting to get my own way, to be right, or to prove my point. But the real battle couples are engaged in is not for such temporal victories. We need to fight for a much larger purpose, such as for the glory of God, the preservation of our marriages, our spiritual health and well-being, and our children's future. The weapons we use to fight these battles must be the weapons God provides—the Word of God and prayer. These weapons are the only ones that have *divine* power to demolish strongholds (2 Corinthians 10:4). Oswald Chambers said that prayer is not the preparation for the battle; prayer *is* the battle.[4] With this in mind, we choose spiritual weapons in order to respond righteously. When we understand who our enemy is and what we are fighting for, then we can better plan how to fight back—by overcoming evil with good. "It is God's will that by doing good you should silence the ignorant talk of foolish men" (1 Peter 2:15).

Righteous Response—Overcoming Evil with Good

What kind of good is powerful enough to overcome evil? One of my favorite scenes from the movie *The Empire Strikes Back* is the one in which young Luke Skywalker fights Darth Vader. Luke represents good, Vader, evil. The battle is fierce. Darth Vader knows that the only way he can win is to get Luke Skywalker to begin to hate. That hate would grow, and evil would win.

God's Word states that we overcome evil with good when we choose to respond to wrongdoing in ways that are godly, righteous, and loving. In other words, we should respond to our spouse's wrongs in ways that are in his or her long-term best interests. God always responds to our wrongdoing in ways that are ultimately for our good, even though his strategies may seem harsh. Sometimes they involve letting us go for a while to learn from our mistakes. At other times he allows us to suffer so that we learn obedience. Or he might directly discipline or rebuke us. God's response is always directed toward our good. His goal is to move us toward personal repentance, restoration, and reconciliation of our relationship with him.

In the Scriptures, Hosea's actions are a perfect example of this kind of good. His wife, Gomer, was an adulteress. Her heart was hard, and she hurt her husband with her chronic unfaithfulness. Hosea didn't blow up and rail on her. Nor did he just ignore her behavior and hope for the best. He confronted her (see Hosea 2), set boundaries on what he would and would not do for her, reconfirmed his love for her, and suffered through the humiliation she brought on him. He did all this for the purpose of bringing Gomer to her senses and gaining the eventual restoration of their relationship. Hosea responded to Gomer's sin with the weapons of truth, love, and righteousness. He overcame evil with good.

Queen Esther also learned to act right when her spouse acted wrong. Her husband, the king, made a terrible decision and signed a law permitting the murder of all the Jews on a designated day. What was Esther to do? She could have reacted by marching right into the king's throne room, demanding to be heard, and telling her husband how stupid he was. Or Esther could have been paralyzed with fear and done nothing. If she kept quiet, at least she would be spared, even though all the Jews would be killed. Esther didn't react, but she did respond. She prayed. She fasted and consulted with advisors who gave her the wisdom she needed to respond rightly. She didn't know what the consequences of her actions would be. She might have lost her life, yet she knew that keeping silent was wrong. Eventually, after much prayer and planning, she told her husband the truth. She revealed that he had been tricked into signing this law by his wicked assistant, Haman. Esther overcame evil with good. It was not only good news for the Jews, but it was also good for her. (See the book of Esther for the full story.)

Maybe you have tried tough love, soft love, talking, praying, and everything in between, and still you believe nothing positive has taken place as a result. Much like David from chapter 1, you have tried your best, and still there is no repentance or improved relationship, just continuous hurt and misery. I want to encourage you: Although you may not see the desired evidence of change, two things are happening that you must not lose sight of. First, remember who your enemy is. *It is not your spouse*. Satan might have your spouse, but don't let him have you. He will have both of you if you react out of your sinful human nature. Paul tells us, "Put to death, therefore, whatever belongs to your earthly nature," and then he goes on to list a host of immoral acts. Further on in that passage he tells us, "But now you must rid yourselves of all such things as these: anger, rage, malice, slander, and filthy language from your lips. Do not lie to each other, since you have taken off your old self with its practices and have put on the new self, which is being renewed in knowledge in the image of its Creator" (Colossians 3:8-10). When we remember that our real enemy is Satan, we do not do good in order to get our spouse to change; we do good so that *we* are not overcome by evil. When our spouse acts wrong, we are going to be tempted to sin. Learning to respond with good helps us not to be overcome by sin. That is definitely good for us, even if our spouse is unresponsive.

The second thing we must remember is that it is God's will for us to be conformed to the image of Christ. Therefore, God will allow difficulties in our lives so that we might be shaped and molded into his character. If we keep this picture in our mind, we can see that it is not our task to mold our spouse; that is God's job. We need to search God's Word and pray that he would give us the wisdom to know the right response in each situation we face. Then by faith, we must do it.

Chapters 4 through 9 will explain specific strategies that, if put into practice, will help you win this battle of overcoming evil with good. The first step in any kind of battle strategy is making sure you are adequately protected.

Destiny

Watch your thoughts; they become words;
Watch your words; they become actions.
Watch your actions; they become habits.
Watch your habits; they become character.[5]

Dear Lord,

I am beginning to see that my reactions to things that happen in my life do not always please you. Help me to stop making excuses. Help me to stop blaming others for my bad reactions. Today I want to stop reacting, and I ask you to teach me how to respond to my spouse in the right way. I'm coming to realize that my real enemy is Satan, who wants to destroy me and my marriage. Lord, help me fight back with your weapons, the weapons of right-

eousness you provide me. Teach me how to respond in truth and love and to overcome evil with good. Help me to repent of my self-centeredness and selfishness, my pride and my stubbornness. Lord, change my heart. Make me more like you, especially in my home.

Amen.

FOUR

GUARD YOUR HEART

All the water in all the oceans cannot sink a ship
unless it gets inside.

EUGENE H. PETERSEN

I don't know much about strategic warfare. I've never played with toy soldiers or had the privilege of serving in our country's military. However, I do know something about winning, as I love to win. I am very competitive. Playing sports and certain types of games teaches us some important lessons about winning and developing the necessary strategies to succeed in life. For example, a good offensive strategy and an equally strong defensive plan are essential; against a formidable opponent, one without the other will result in defeat. This was illustrated to one of my clients by an event at her son's soccer game. The boys had a great offensive team but a weak goalie. Their opponents scored a huge number of goals. The opposing team was not a better team, but without an adequate defense, her son's team had no hope of winning the game.

In any kind of warfare, we must make provisions to protect ourselves from becoming mortally wounded. God tells us in his wisdom,

"Above all else, guard your heart, for it is the wellspring of life" (Proverbs 4:23). Our heart (which includes or encompasses our mind, our emotions, and our will) must be protected against anything that would distract us from or threaten our commitment to Christ and our love and trust in him. Satan will either batter us or beguile us into walking away from Christ. Because he, not our spouse, is the true enemy, we must be mindful of his strategies and the weapons he uses to throw us off course.

Know Your Enemy

My husband is a very good volleyball coach. In addition to teaching his team skills, offensive strategies, and defensive plays, he studies other teams. He spends time observing their players, their positions, their strategies, and their strengths and weaknesses. The better he understands the enemy, the less vulnerable his team is to defeat.

Satan doesn't vary his strategies much. What worked with people throughout the Scriptures works today as well. We need to know Satan's schemes so that we are not taken in by his deceptiveness. I discussed some of the mental obstacles that trip us up in our marriage in chapter 1. Satan will often use seemingly truthful statements ("It's not fair," "I just want to be happy") to direct our attention toward our spouse or our felt needs. His strategy is to take what looks true and then twist it ever so slightly until it is no longer the full truth but a distortion of the truth. He is a deceiver (John 8:44), and one of his most effective strategies is to cleverly disguise his lies, making them look like truth.

I once overheard a discussion my two children had about the devil. Ryan was telling his younger sister, Amanda, that the devil makes himself look good to people so that they will follow and believe him. Amanda looked puzzled. Ryan continued, "If the devil looked like who he really was, everyone would be too scared of him." Amanda nodded with understanding.

Satan does indeed behave in this way. He did this when he began his work on Eve in the garden. (See Genesis 3.) God warned Adam and Eve that if they ate from the tree of knowledge, they would die. Satan challenged God's warning by saying, "You will not surely die" and implied that God forbade the eating of the tree because the fruit would cause them to become like God. *God wants to gyp you out of something good, Eve.* She began to believe what Satan said more than what God had said. Our natural tendency is to believe what we want to hear rather than to believe the truth. (See Romans 1.) Satan is only too happy to whisper what we want to hear.

Another favorite strategy of Satan is to appeal to our *felt needs* rather than to our deeper or true needs. For example, in the desert temptation, Satan appealed to Jesus' hunger (felt need). Satan also appealed to Christ's desire to be acknowledged as God's chosen one. Can you picture Satan taunting Jesus? "If you are the Son of God, tell this stone to become bread" (Luke 4:3). *Prove yourself, Jesus! Feed yourself, Jesus!* How very tempting it must have been for Jesus—hot, hungry, vulnerable. In a flash Jesus could have turned those dusty desert stones into warm crusty bread, satisfying his hunger and proving he was indeed the Son of God.

How many times does Satan come at us the same way when we are tired, vulnerable, and emotionally hungry? *Go ahead, your husband isn't meeting your needs for love and appreciation. God wants you to be happy.* Or what about, *Hey, you have rights too. Why should you be the only one who is giving in this marriage?* Satan would love to deceive us into thinking that when we are hungry (either physically, emotionally, or sexually), we must meet those needs ourselves even if it means sinning. *Don't wait,* he purrs. *Don't trust God. God helps those who help themselves.* Waiting and trusting God are difficult to do, especially when the opportunity to meet our felt needs is presented right beneath our noses, as it was for Jesus. Thankfully, Jesus was on guard against the schemes of Satan and knew his strategies. He did not sinfully meet his own needs; he trusted God to provide. We, too, need to follow Christ's example.

Another one of Satan's favorite schemes is to trick us into thinking the sin our spouse has committed against us or our children is so great that it is unforgivable. Stuart sinned against his family in one of the most grievous ways by committing incest with his daughter. Marnie, his wife, was beside herself with grief and rage. "I'll never forgive what you've done," she wept bitterly. Marnie's feelings were a normal reaction to such a horrible act. Yet if Marnie wants to deal with this offense as Christ would have her to, she will eventually need to face the forgiveness issue as Stuart demonstrates the fruits of real repentance.

The apostle Paul faced a similar situation at the church at Corinth when he discovered incest. It appalled him. This offense was not to be ignored or swept under the carpet. Church discipline brought the offender to repentance. Over time, however, love was to be restored. Evil was to be overcome with good. It was good that they confronted the offender. It was good that they disciplined him in order to bring him to repentance. Paul said, "I urge you, therefore, to reaffirm your love for him." He went on to state, "I have forgiven in the sight of Christ for your sake, in order that Satan might not outwit us. For we are not unaware of his schemes" (2 Corinthians 2:8,10-11).

Satan might use other people to throw us off course. He used Potiphar's wife to tempt Joseph into abandoning his allegiance to God (Genesis 39). He used Jezebel to scare the daylights out of Elijah right after a great spiritual victory (1 Kings 19). As Jesus was talking with his disciples about his impending death, Satan used Peter to attempt to dissuade Jesus from the cross. "Never, Lord!" Peter cried. "This shall never happen to you." Though Peter meant well, Satan tried to use him to entice Christ to move away from God's plan. Satan did this by tempting Christ toward the sin of pride, implying, *Jesus, you're much too valuable here to waste yourself dying on the cross as a martyr.* Jesus' response to Peter may appear harsh but was correct: "'Get behind me, Satan,' he said. 'You do not have in mind the things of God, but the things of men'" (Mark 8:33).

At times people will tell us just the things we want to hear: In fact, if we are not careful, we will actively look for people who do. Recently a woman whom I was counseling became angry with me. She felt I was trying to convince her to stay married even though she wanted to divorce her husband. "I just don't have feelings for him anymore," she said. "Why should I give up the rest of my life for a promise I made when I was too young and stupid to know what I was doing?" When I talked to her about what God wants for her, she bristled. Isaiah tells us that there will be "children unwilling to listen to the LORD's instruction. They say to the seers, 'See no more visions!' and to the prophets, 'Give us no more visions of what is right! Tell us pleasant things, prophesy illusions. Leave this way, get off this path, and stop confronting us with the Holy One of Israel!'" (Isaiah 30:9-11). Satan is only too willing to provide people who will "tell us pleasant things." This client stopped coming to me and found another counselor who told her what she wanted to hear.

Guard Your Heart Against Sinful Feelings

Normal feelings such as hurt, sadness, anger, and disappointment occur in every marriage. We need not be stoic in bearing up under difficulties. Jesus himself "mourned and wept for his own calamities as well as for those of others, and He did not teach his disciples any different way."[1] God does not expect us to endure our marital difficulties with cheerfulness. That would be silly. Yet within these difficult and painful emotions, God *does* want us to guard our heart against the hardness of heart, bitterness, vengeance, or hopelessness that can result from being in a difficult marriage. Bitterness grows out of unforgiveness, discouragement out of chronic hurt. Apathy or a desire for revenge grows out of unchecked pride and anger. Holding on to these feelings builds walls of resentment and hardness of heart that makes it impossible to love. When our spouse acts wrong and we do not learn to respond rightly to the circumstances, we will begin to apply defensive layers to our heart. They may appear quite thin at first, but if not regularly removed, they will harden into thick walls of self-protection that later seem impenetrable.

Beth was charming and fun. Everyone enjoyed her humor and quick wit, although it was often at the expense of her husband, Stephen. In the beginning, he took her jabs without rancor, even laughing with her. Over time he grew tired of being the target of her attention-getting antics. He began resenting her and withdrawing. Stephen was protecting himself in a destructive way. Instead of confronting Beth's behavior or sharing with her his hurt and anger, he withdrew and built walls cemented with resentment and bitterness around his heart. Satan got a foothold (Ephesians 4:27) in Stephen's life and would win this battle if Stephen didn't get a better strategy for guarding his heart.

Guard Your Heart Against Fear and Worry

Jesus tells us: "Are not two sparrows sold for a penny? Yet not one of them will fall to the ground apart from the will of your Father. And even the very hairs on your head are all numbered. So don't be afraid; you are worth more than many sparrows" (Matthew 10:29-31). Fear can paralyze us or propel us into foolish action. We need to guard our heart against the fear perpetrated by an overactive imagination that tends to always picture the worst possible scenario. God instructs us to deal with our fears by trusting him. The apostle Paul tells us that when we are anxious we should pray (Philippians 4:4-7). Our prayers cannot bring us any peace, however, unless we *believe* God; we must believe that he hears and that he cares. A heart of fear will keep us focused on how to stay safe rather than on how to trust or please God. The Israelites missed an opportunity to enter the Promised Land because they feared the giants instead of believing what God told them (Numbers 13-14).

Heather struggled with whether to confront her husband with his lies about where he spent his time and their money. She suspected he might be involved with another woman but wasn't sure. Fear gripped her heart. "What is going to happen if he gets mad? What if it's true and he wants a divorce?" After much prayer, she finally told me, "I saw I had a real choice, Leslie. I could live in a world of fear or a world of faith. God gave me the grace to jump into the world of faith. I would have to learn to totally trust him." With that resolve, Heather confronted her husband with the evidence and trusted God with the outcome.

Guard Your Heart Against Discouragement

Peter loved Jesus. He wanted to serve Christ and follow him. Peter was even willing to die for him. Never did Peter think he would waver from allowing Christ to be number one in his life. Yet Peter did. What happened? Jesus disappointed him. Jesus didn't respond to his arrest in the way Peter thought he should. Peter never dreamed Jesus would willingly and without a fight hand himself over to his captors. He and the other disciples were so sure of the ensuing battle that when the crowd came to arrest Jesus, the disciples reached for their swords, and Peter even cut off the ear of the high priest's servant. Jesus' response was to forbid the disciples to fight, and he reached out and healed the wounded man's ear (John 18:10-11; Matthew 26:47-52). Peter was confused. He was discouraged. He didn't get it. He thought Christ was going to be their king. Instead, he willingly yielded himself when arrested and didn't even defend himself.

This kind of confusion and discouragement can happen to us, too. We are doing well. Our faith is strong. We are handling our difficulties with our spouse by trusting God. Then *wham!* Disappointment blindsides us. God doesn't answer our prayers in the way we expected him to. He doesn't heal our marriage or cause our spouse to repent.

Like David from chapter 1, we can be deceived by Satan into believing that nothing is happening, especially when we are trying very hard to live according to God's Word. Let's learn a lesson from Peter to guard our heart against discouragement. Let God be God. Trust him to know what is best, even when we don't understand.

Guard Your Heart Against Pretense or a Peace-at-Any-Price Mentality

For the more tender-hearted among us, the thought of any kind of warfare is completely unnerving. Jesus' words "Blessed are the peace-makers" are more soothing. But if we want to have any true or lasting peace, we must be willing to enter into battle at times.

The Hebrew word for peace is *shalom*. This word implies much more than the absence of war or conflict. "Implicit in *shalom* is the idea of unimpaired relationships with others and fulfillment in one's under-takings."[2] Oswald Chambers warns us to "be careful that you do not obtain inner peace and unity at the Devil's price. Obtain them as Christ bestows them, through the alteration of your sinful disposition through the Holy Spirit."[3] If you want to learn to act right when your spouse acts wrong, you will need to make a commitment to yourself never to pretend that things are fine when they are not. That does not mean we should bring up every little injustice that our spouse commits or every little irritant that ruffles our feathers. However, we must be honest with ourselves about the current state of affairs.

Several years back my family and I sat huddled around our television set one early Saturday morning to watch an extraordinary event. Corporate Plaza Office Building, an eight-year-old multimillion-dollar office complex in downtown Allentown was about to come crashing down on itself and disappear into a cloud of dust, imploding into oblivion.

Just a few weeks earlier everything appeared normal. People worked in the building as usual, preparing for the busy tax season. Huge glass windowpanes sparkled with the winter's sunshine. Everything on the outside looked ordinary, even peaceful, considering all the snow we had that year. Little did anyone know or suspect that deep beneath the foundation of that building a problem of enormous implications was developing. A sinkhole had formed and had begun to expand, eroding an area over eighteen feet deep and fifty feet wide.

The first clue that something was wrong came when the operators of the city's reservoir system noticed a significant drop in water levels in the middle of the night. Their investigation revealed the widening sinkhole. Shortly after that discovery, huge shards of glass and bricks began to tumble to the pavement below as the building buckled and cracked, teetering on the verge of collapse. The damage was so severe that the entire building had to be demolished for the safety of the community.

Corporate Plaza was destroyed by a force identified too late to reverse the damage. Like Corporate Plaza, our marriage might appear to be perfectly fine. We look good to outside observers. Perhaps we even tell ourselves that all is well. Yet a menacing sinkhole is developing at the very foundation of our marriage, a sinkhole of apathy or boredom, resentment or discontent. It may develop gradually, but it will destroy our marriage if we do not pay attention and address the problem. We must be careful. When we pretend nothing is wrong, problems don't go away.

How Can We Guard Our Heart?

To answer this question, we must turn our attention away from our enemy and toward God. It is not enough to know Satan's tricks, strategies, and schemes; we must also listen to God to overcome them. Proverbs offers us some important guidelines for our protection.

For wisdom will enter your heart,
  and knowledge will be pleasant to your soul.
Discretion will protect you,
  and understanding will guard you.
Wisdom will save you from the ways of wicked men,
  from men whose words are perverse. (Proverbs 2:10-12)

Do not forsake wisdom, and she will protect you;
  love her, and she will watch over you. (Proverbs 4:6)

Hold on to instruction, do not let it go;
  guard it well, for it is your life. (Proverbs 4:13)

My son, pay attention to what I say;
  listen closely to my words.
Do not let them out of your sight,
  keep them within your heart;
for they are life to those who find them
  and health to a man's whole body.
Above all else, guard your heart,
  for it is the wellspring of life. (Proverbs 4:20-23)

The highway of the upright avoids evil;
  he who guards his way guards his life. (Proverbs 16:17)

In order to guard our heart effectively, we must not only know what God is saying; we must also believe him. The movie *Life Is Beautiful* illustrated this truth to me in a most powerful way. The story is about a young Jewish boy and his father, who have been taken to a concentration camp during World War II. Throughout this ordeal, the father kept the son from experiencing the horror of the concentration camp by telling him that things were not as they appeared. They were at a special camp and were playing a game. The prize? A great big tank, which they would win if they could earnestly keep all the rules. The boy's father oriented him toward this goal and kept his eyes on the prize.

At times the young boy was discouraged and tempted to give up. He didn't like this game. He got hungry. He didn't like having to hide under the bedcovers all the time. He heard terrible things—people were being turned into soap and buttons. Each time the boy was tempted to give up, the father would frantically remind him, "We're going to win, Son. Just a little longer, we're almost there." In spite of all manner of evil that was surrounding this little boy, it did not penetrate his soul. Why not? Because he believed his father, he trusted in his words. The child was kept sane in the midst of an insane situation because he loved his dad and kept his attention riveted on what his father was telling him, even with overwhelming evidence to the contrary.

Our heavenly Father does the same thing for us, with one huge difference. In spite of his good intentions, the father in *Life Is Beautiful* was not telling his boy the truth. But our heavenly Father does not lie (Titus 1:2). The writer of Hebrews assures us that because God doesn't lie and doesn't change, we have an anchor for our soul (Hebrews 6:18-19). A. W. Tozer says, "True faith rests upon the character of God and asks no further proof than the moral perfections of the

One who cannot lie. It is enough that God said it, and if the statement should contradict every one of the five senses and all the conclusions of logic as well, still the believer continues to believe."[4]

We can only guard our heart and learn how to act right when our spouse acts wrong if we believe and trust what God tells us. Chuck Swindoll says, "The wonderful thing about relying on God's Book is that it gives you stability." He adds, "No other counsel will get you through the long haul. No other truth will help you to stand firm in the storms of doubt and uncertainty. No other reality will give you strength for each day and deep hope for tomorrow. No other instruction has the power to give new meaning to your life."[5]

Guarding your heart with truth isn't just believing a set of principles within God's Word; it is believing and trusting a Person. Jesus tells us that he is the truth (John 14:6) and that he is telling us the truth (he tells us this repeatedly throughout the Gospels). "We begin to recognize lies when we know the Truth."[6] Beth Moore advises us, "The fastest way to lose our balance in warfare is to rebuke the devil more than we relate to God. The primary strength we have in warfare is godliness, which is achieved only through intimacy with God."[7]

Our relationship with our spouse may be shaky and out of control, but God is always near and willingly hears our cries. Oswald Chambers tells us to "guard jealously your relationship to God"[8] for he is our one absolutely true thing in life. God doesn't change or waver. He is steadfast and strong, even when we feel weak and our feet slip. He is like the lighthouse that sailors search for in the fog; he is the one sure thing. Sailors know if they don't quickly orient themselves according to the lighthouse, they will most certainly become lost or shipwrecked. In order not to become confused in the fog of marital distress, we must make sure we are spending quality time talking and listening to God. God protects and guards our heart—with himself.

Lord Jesus,

Guard my heart. Sometimes I allow Satan to deceive and trick me into abandoning your purposes in my life. At times I pay more attention to my pain or my temporal happiness than your glory, and Satan uses those things to make me think that your ways can't be trusted or are not good. Jesus, give me the faith to believe you, not just believe in you. I long for my life to be more like yours was—a life of absolute trust in the Father. Give me strength to apply the things I am learning so that I might reflect you in my home, especially when my spouse isn't acting as I'd like. Give my husband/wife eyes to see and ears to hear when you speak to his/her heart. Help me to let go of my agenda for what should happen and how things should work out. I want to trust you more completely. Lord, guard my heart and mind against anything that would thwart your purposes in my life.

Amen.

FIVE

CENTER YOURSELF IN GOD

In him we live and move and have our being.

ACTS 17:28

As Gary and I concluded our counseling session, I closed with prayer, as is my habit. When we were done, Gary reached for his briefcase and sighed, "Now, off to the real world." I paused for a moment and then gently said, "No, Gary. We were just *in* the real world; the world you are returning to is false. It is full of lies. It is a make-believe world that Satan creates to tempt you to believe that life and happiness are to be found in it. The *real* world is Christ." (See Colossians 2:17.)

Like Gary, what many of us experience in life seems much more real to us than what we experience in our spiritual life. God, the Bible, and the way of living that we've been talking about seem nice but unrealistic. Sometimes I hear, "Hey, Leslie, get real," meaning, "How can I possibly believe that the things we've been talking about are possible?"

There's truth in this question. We will not be able to do any of the things I've discussed so far if our relationship with God isn't the central passion in our life. Our relationship with him must be our truest reality. If Christianity is just a Sunday sort of thing, if our Bible is something we keep in a drawer only to pull out when we need it, or if our faith consists of nothing more than a nice set of religious principles, then none of these will seem adequate to sustain us when the difficulties of married life threaten our well-being. "If you don't believe in heaven, divorce can make a lot of sense."[1]

All of Scripture echoes the theme that this world, with its pleasures and its pains, is only a temporary place. "In ordinary life, we are tempted to measure things subjectively: in terms of earthly success, achieving our goals, or fulfilling someone else's expectations. But our lives have depth and meaning only when we view them from a higher vantage point, when we measure our temporal concerns against the eternal now."[2]

God created us for eternity and for a deep abiding fellowship with him. There is an ache in our soul that only God can fill. God designed our heart to worship; therefore, we will center our heart in those things or persons we deem most worthy of our love, attention, energy, and resources. To worship something is to value it above anything and everything else. It is to honor and revere it. Whether we are intentional about it or not, we all center ourselves in what we worship. Our center defines us. It reveals who we are and what we live for.

As Christians, many of us think God is our center. But, truth be told, we center ourselves in other things—even good things like a satisfying marriage or personal happiness. Although these other things are not sinful, if they remain at our center, we will never be able to act right when that center is threatened. Jesus lamented, "These people honor me with their lips, but their hearts are far from me" (Matthew 15:8). Jesus knew that whatever was at the center of our heart, centered us. He said, "For where your treasure is, there your heart will be also" (Matthew 6:21).

Our center is where we go to find peace, happiness, and refuge. It is what we anchor ourselves to in the midst of a storm. It becomes our rock, the belief we stand on, the hope we cling to, the "defining sphere of our existence."³ Sadly, many of us, even believers, anchor ourselves to a deceptive or unreliable center. The Scriptures teach that some have taken refuge in a lie—temporarily (Isaiah 28:15). Sometimes knowingly and sometimes ignorantly, we have centered ourselves in falsehoods, the lies of this world that will not only compromise our marital relationship, but will also ultimately threaten our very well-being and happiness.

The Lie of Self-Centeredness
(the Worship of Self)

We are born self-centered. That is original sin. We are intrinsically and naturally inclined to believe the lie that *we* are the center of everything or that life revolves around us. The very center of pride is *I*. When we buy into this lie, our source of truth and life-giving reality becomes what we want, what we think, and what we feel. We will desire to be worshiped, loved, praised, adored, and in control of everything. For a child to grow into an emotionally healthy person who has the capacity to love and be loved, her bubble of omnipotence must be popped as she faces the disappointment of discovering a reality larger than herself. Even in this temporal world, a child must descend from her pedestal and accept the painful truth that she is a mere human being.

We have all met adults who have not learned this or have not realized it fully. They still think that the world and other people should revolve around them, their needs, their desires, their wants, and their feelings. They make terrible marriage partners, as they have little capacity to empathize with their spouse or to give love without demanding something in return. They are selfish and often controlling. At times they may groan, "I hate reality." Why? Because they do not like to face their own sinfulness, smallness, and neediness. They would rather be god.

Some of us may be further along in this process but still cling to remnants of centering ourselves in what *we* think we need for life instead of in believing what God tells us we need. Some of the mental obstacles listed in chapter 1 reveal the struggle we have with genuinely believing God rather than our own feelings when he tells us what will bring us life. When in doubt, we often believe ourselves before we believe God.

That's why many people jump ship in their marriage when it gets hard. We don't really believe God when he tells us that these hardships can and will be used for our good. We don't believe him when he tells us that *he* is our deepest source of satisfaction and joy. Instead, we live for pleasure, for the moment, for the gratification of our sensual desires, or for whatever else we think will bring us happiness and fulfillment. "There is a deep and very old voice in [us] that whispers that God can't be trusted with anything so important as [our] life. That fear is the root of sin. It moves [us] to believe that life is only what [we] make it. Gripped by that anxiety, [we] fear that [we] will not get the respect [we] want or the accomplishments and possessions [we] think [we] deserve unless [we] grab as much as [we] can and feverishly protect it."[4]

Sometimes we deceive ourselves into believing that we are God-centered because the things around which we orient our lives (church, ministries, work, family) are good things. Like David from chapter 1, we can do all the right things but for the wrong reasons. Our behaviors may look Christlike, but our heart is centered in ourselves and in getting what we want and think we need for life. The fruit might look a little different, but the roots of self-centeredness are the same. Paul cautions us against this self-orientation. He tells us, "Each of you should look not only to your own interests, but also to the interests of others" (Philippians 2:4). Self-centeredness is quite automatic and natural in all of us. If we are to grow in Christ, we will need to consciously choose to die to ourselves and to purposely center ourselves in Someone greater.

The Lie of Other-Centeredness (the Worship of Others)

Frantic, Susan called me to make an appointment for herself and her husband. "We have to see you immediately," she cried. "George just told me that he is in love with another woman and he's planning to move out. He has agreed to one counseling session. How soon can you see us?" Susan pinned all her hopes on my being able to change George's mind. Of course, he had already made up his mind. I was not going to change it in one session.

"Tell me what I need to do differently to be more of what you want," Susan pleaded as George sat stone-faced. "I'll do anything, just tell me!" Finally in desperation, Susan sobbed, "Don't leave me, I *need* you. Please, just love me." Susan's pain was intense and difficult to watch. She felt as if she were dying. The person she had centered herself in was leaving, and she felt she was losing the inner core that defined her life. Her heart was breaking, not only because of the self-centered actions of her husband, but because her heart was empty. Susan believed the lie of other-centeredness, whereby you live to gain and keep the love and approval of others. Her husband was her center—her defining sphere of existence, her reason to be. When he no longer loved her or wanted her as a wife, she crumbled. Susan lost not only her husband and her marriage; she lost herself.

The apostle Paul warns us in Romans 1 that we will quite naturally exchange the truth of God for a lie and we will tend to worship and serve created things instead of God, the Creator of all things. The lie that we will find ultimate happiness and fulfillment by gaining the love and approval of certain others will always cause us to stumble. If we tell ourselves we can only feel happy when someone (whom we deem important) loves us and thinks we're worth something, what happens when they don't love us anymore or don't think we're worth anything? Does that mean we aren't?

I have met many people who live in perpetual hurt and disappointment because someone they value doesn't love them in the manner they seek. There are adults who still try to win or earn the love and approval they never got from their parents. Others bend over backward trying to please people so that no one will ever be angry or disappointed with them and everyone will love them. They attempt to anticipate everyone's need ahead of time so that they can meet the need and feel important or necessary. Their fear of people is more powerful than their fear of God (Proverbs 29:25; Isaiah 51:7-13; John 12:43).

Ultimately we will have to choose whether we are going to be people-pleasers or God-pleasers (Galatians 1:10). Often as Christians we are taught to put others first, but God does not want us to be other-centered people; he wants us to be God-centered people. Whenever we put anything or anyone other than God at the center of our heart, we will find ourselves bending in an unnatural and unhealthy posture, leaning into lies or illusions that promise us life but deliver something far less. Job reminds us that when we trust in anything other than God, it is about as reliable as leaning against a spider's web (Job 8:13-15). Such things are extremely fragile and can disappear in an instant.

An equally destructive problem occurs when we allow others to put us at the center of their lives. Once I had a friend who tried to make me her god. She didn't state this directly, but what she wanted was for me to fulfill her and make her feel whole, loved, and needed. In my own naive grandiosity, I stupidly tried to comply with her wishes. I promised that I would be there for her—meaning I would unconditionally love her, care for her, and show her how valuable and worthwhile she was. I honestly tried, but I failed—miserably! I could never be god for her; only God can be God. He is the only one who is perfectly patient, perfectly pure, perfectly loving, perfectly just, perfectly everything. God does not want us to center ourselves in loving others or having others love us. Although it sounds good and true, it is still a lie. As we center our heart in God and learn to love him with all of our heart, soul, mind, and strength, he equips us to love others with a supernatural kind of love—his love. Loving others well comes out of loving him first. I have learned that the best I can do is be a reflection of him to others, an example of him. I can never *be* him.

The Truth of God-Centeredness
(the Worship of Yahweh)

Centering ourselves in God means collecting all that is scattered around us—our misplaced trust, our disordered desires, our emotions, thoughts, problems—and yielding them to God. It means allowing God to take his rightful place in our life by giving ourselves entirely to him. The most important love relationship is not the one between a husband and a wife but the one between God and the human soul. The psalmist described this longing when he said, "As the deer pants for streams of water, so my soul pants for you, O God" (Psalm 42:1). When our relationship with God is right, "we won't make such severe demands on our marriage, asking each other, expecting each other, to compensate for spiritual emptiness."[5]

We can learn to act right when our spouse acts wrong because we are not impoverished, standing before our spouse with empty hands. We can give out of our abundance because we are full—not full of marital bliss but full of God. He is the best spouse (Isaiah 54:5).

Knowing God

We will never be able to center ourselves in God or truly worship him if we do not know him. Part of the process of Christian maturity is to transform our faith from head knowledge into heartfelt trust. Trusting God is far more than mentally acknowledging the reality of God; it is learning to rely on him. We come to trust him to be enough for us. The apostle John reminds us of this process of maturity when he says, "And so we know and *rely* on the love God has for us" (1 John 4:16). God will use our marital difficulties (as well as other troubles in life) to draw our heart toward knowing him, not just knowing something about him or a set of theological principles.

In Luke 8 we read the familiar story of Jesus calming the raging storm. At first glance we may merely view this story as one of many that illustrate Jesus is indeed God. Yet in it, Jesus was teaching his disciples a deeper lesson. Jesus wanted them to know who he was *and* that they could absolutely rely on him. The disciples thought they knew Jesus, but after Jesus calmed the churning sea with a mere word, they turned wide-eyed to one another in amazement and fear and cried, "Who is this man?" They realized they didn't really know him as they thought they did. Just like the disciples, sometimes in the midst of our own personal storms we, too, come to realize that we don't know him as well as we thought we did or as well as we need to. As we cry out for help, God often answers our prayers in such a way as to bring us into a deeper awareness of who he is so that we can come to fully rely on him.

If you could ask God for just one thing—anything you desire right now—and know that he would grant your request, what would you ask him for? Would your prayer be, "Lord, I just want to know you more"? (See Psalm 27:4.) Many of us ask God for good things. Please don't misunderstand; he wants us to bring each and every need we have before him. However, many of us don't realize that the thing we need *most* in this life, after forgiveness, is to know God. He is our only true source of love and life. The apostle Paul prayed that he might know God. Paul wanted nothing more in this life than to know his Lord more fully (Philippians 3:10). John Piper says, "Christ, the essence and image of God, is more to be desired than all his gifts. He is the end of our soul's savoring, not the means."[6] Oswald Chambers reminds us, "Eternal life is not a gift from God, eternal life is the gift *of God*."[7] Jesus prays, "Now this is eternal life: that they may know you, the only true God, and Jesus Christ, whom you have sent" (John 17:3). God yearns for us to know him. He longs for us to *want* to know him. Tozer says, "He waits to be wanted. Too bad that with many of us He waits so long, so very long, in vain."[8] When we have no growing desire to know God, we ought to question the validity of our professed faith. Is it in God or just in a set of ideas or principles?

God compares our relationship with him to a marriage. We are the bride; he is the groom. (See Isaiah 54:5 and Revelation 21:2.) We are in him; he is in us. (See Jesus' prayer for believers starting in John 17:20.) He compares our relationship with him to the deepest kind of marital oneness. In a good marriage there is sexual intimacy, love, trust, and commitment. "In a happy home the husband doesn't talk to the wife only when he wants something from her. He doesn't pop in only when he wants a good meal or a clean shirt or a little romance. If he does, the home is not a home—it's a brothel that serves food and cleans clothes."[9] Often, instead of enjoying God or even knowing him for who he is, we *use* him as a means to get our more important desires or felt needs met. This deeply hurts him, because he wants to be the love of our life and the consuming desire of our heart. "Saving faith is the heartfelt conviction not only that Christ is reliable, but also that he is desirable. It is the confidence that he will come through with his promises *and* that what he promises is more to be desired than all the world."[10]

Our Other Loves

Lucy and Ernie had been married a long time, but in recent years they encountered some troubles that threatened to end their marriage. Lucy said she loved Ernie, but she also had some male "friends" on the side that she met through the Internet. She wanted to stay married to Ernie, but she didn't want to give up her other lovers. She said they made her feel alive, as if she was somebody important. Ernie loved Lucy but would not share her with other men. He wanted to be her only love. He was deeply hurt when Lucy didn't value him or their marital relationship as much as she valued the ego boost she got from having her other lovers. God is a jealous God. He does not want us to have other lovers. When we insist, we will forfeit our intimacy with him. "The first and greatest commandment is to love God with every power of our entire being. Where love like that exists there can be no place for a second object."[11] God will never force us into a relationship with him, but he will not share us either. (For a greater picture of this, read the book of Hosea.) Our unfaithfulness hurts and saddens him. It breaks his heart (Ezekiel 6:9).

Many of us give lip service to loving God even though other loves take first place in our heart. Again, our loves might not be sinful in and of themselves, such as loving a good marriage, loving obedient children, loving a clean and orderly home, or loving financial security. However, when we *must* have these things for our well-being, when we feel God is insufficient, then these desires have become idols and have taken first place in our heart. These other loves, no matter how good and legitimate they are, compromise our intimacy with God.[12]

Loving God

At one point in my life, intimacy with God was something I didn't understand very well. My faith was based on rules I felt compelled to obey or principles I mentally agreed with. Prayer was my means of getting something from God, not a pathway to God himself. To be passionate with God and about God seemed weird. I didn't understand it, let alone know how to achieve it. Much like a marriage relationship, intimacy with God will not be achieved if we don't spend time with him, honestly talking with him, listening to him, and building trust by valuing and believing what he tells us. Even if we do all that, it is possible to still miss one more important ingredient. God wants us to find our greatest pleasure in loving him and him alone. John Piper says, "Loving God may include obeying all his commands; it may include believing all his Word; it may include thanking him for all his gifts; but the essence of loving God is enjoying all he is. It is this enjoyment of God that glorifies his worth most fully, especially when all around our soul gives way."[13]

How would you feel if you were married to someone who talked to you and did what you asked for but only out of a sense of duty? What if he or she found no pleasure in your company? Many of us are like that in the presence of God. We attend worship services because we're supposed to, but we barely participate. We have our morning devotions but find no pleasure in sitting at Jesus' feet. We express more passion watching a television program, participating in a sport, or going to the shopping mall than we do singing a great hymn honoring the King of kings and Lord of lords. When was the last time you were overwhelmed by God—not by what he did but by who he is? C. S. Lewis says, "We are half-hearted creatures, fooling about with drink and sex and ambition when infinite joy is offered us, like an ignorant child who wants to go on making mud pies in a slum because he cannot imagine what is meant by the offer of a holiday at the sea. We are far too easily pleased."[14] God desires to be known, and he desires to be loved by his people. We will love and worship what most deeply impresses our heart. Sadly, often it is not God that most deeply wows our soul. Temporal delights seem much more satisfying and desirable than the things of God.

The psalmist declared, "Your love is better than life" (Psalm 63:3). Centering our heart in God means that we believe God is the most desirable, enjoyable pursuit we have. Therefore, we will not allow anything to take the place of our relationship with him or to relegate him to second place in our heart. This is especially crucial when we struggle in a marriage that may be difficult. If our central passion is ourselves or even a good marriage, we will unwittingly let other desires—such as the desire for happiness, fairness, love, and consideration—rule our heart instead of the love of Christ.

As we center our heart in God, we learn to acknowledge and accept his sovereign control over every circumstance in our life—including our marriage. God never promises us that we will not experience troubles in this life; in fact, he tells us just the opposite (John 16:33). He never tells us that nothing will ever hurt us or that we should look for the easiest way out of our difficulties. God promises this: First, that he will take every difficulty we encounter, including difficulties in our marriage, and transform them into something that will help us to become more like Jesus, which he tells us is very, very good (Romans 8:28-29). Second, he promises that nothing that happens to us will *ever* be able to separate us from his love (Romans 8:38-39). *Ever!* He is in control and always sees the big picture.

Recently one of my former clients shared with me how much she enjoyed my book *The TRUTH Principle*. She said, "I got so much out of your book because I already knew you—it made it more real." Then she blushed and added, "I guess that's how it should be with God when I read the Bible." She's absolutely right. The more we know, love, and enjoy God, the more his Word comes alive. It isn't just a book of stories or rules to live by, it is a heartfelt love letter written by God to us that wonderfully satisfies our soul. Jeremiah said, "When your words came, I ate them; they were my joy and my heart's delight" (Jeremiah 15:16).

God's Glory—Our Centering Passion

All of life's decisions are made from our center. If God is not the centering force in our life, we will never be able to act right when our spouse acts wrong. It is just too difficult to train ourselves in his ways if he is not who and what we love the *most*. If we love him, we will obey him (John 14:15,23). Obedience is God's love language. Acting right when our spouse acts wrong requires us to yield ourselves to God's perspective of life and God's purposes in our life. It calls us to learn how to respond in his way when we are mistreated, not to react in our own ways. We can only do this when we love God more than we love ourselves. Because of this love relationship, we are willing to yield ourselves as a living sacrifice to be used by God to bring him glory (Romans 12:1).

We need to begin living at the point where everything, and nothing short of that, is about the glory of God. That is the end for which we were made (Isaiah 43:6-7) and, as Christians, that is the end for which we should live (1 Corinthians 10:31). Yet many of us have made an exchange. We have devalued living for God's glory and have valued living for something else as our ultimate satisfaction in life. For many of us, the shift has been subtle but the erosion steady.

An athlete who is talented but not centered in his or her sport will never be an Olympian. In order to attain that dream, he or she must center his or her life in that prize. What he eats, when she sleeps, which exercises he will do all revolve around one thing—winning the gold. That is the metaphor the apostle Paul uses in 1 Corinthians 9:24-25 when he tells us to train, to run, to make every effort to live a life that pleases God.

No one forces an athlete to become an Olympian. Some parents might pressure their children to participate in sports, just as others pressure their children to attend church. But a true Olympian has a fire within, a centering force that orients his or her life toward one goal. The choice an athlete makes is because of his desire to win. No one can force us to center our heart in God, not even God. It is a free choice. As believers, we live in two worlds, the temporal and the eternal. Which world is your reality?

By definition, we orient our life around what we are centered in. If we are centered in ourselves or our temporary happiness, it does not matter what religious beliefs we claim to hold; we will make choices based on our true core values. When God is our center, the same is true: No matter what happens to us, our response will come out of what is truly at our core. If we want happiness and contentment in life, we must center ourselves in God and not in our self, our spouse, or any other created person or thing. It is only through holiness and righteousness that we will find happiness, and true happiness cannot be found apart from centering ourselves in Christ. "For from him and through him and to him are all things. To him be the glory forever!" (Romans 11:36). This is the truest truth we can know.

The Eagle Psalm

Lord Jesus, You are everywhere, every when and every place

You are in and through everything
You are the cause and the purpose
You are the path and the goal
You are the light we see by
You are the hand in the dark places

You are the burning crackling fire
You are the cool running waters
You are the wind that sets us free

You are the rock and the foundation
You are the cleft where we hide
You are the cliff from which we fly

You are the one who lines our nest with comfort

You are the one who launches us unsuspectingly
    into the frightening turbulence of Your Presence

You are the one who glides beneath us
    as we plummet to our doom

You are the one on whom we fall
    before we shatter on the rocks

You are the one who carries us back to safety
    on the edge of the precipice

You are the one who pushes us out again and again
    until we know in the very core of our being
    that soaring in the winds is our purpose
    and our great delight

You are the joy of no limitations

Because You are the only limit we have
    —L. M. Miles[15]

Dear Lord,

Forgive me for allowing other things—good things and bad things—to squeeze you from your rightful place at the center of my heart. You deserve first place, and today I yield myself to you as fully as I know how. Each day teach me more of your ways, Lord. Help me to develop the eyes to see and ears to hear what you call me to do in response to difficulties I encounter in my marriage. Lord, I confess that I have too often been self-centered or other-centered and more passionate about pleasing myself or others than pleasing you.

Lord, I desire to see the bigger spiritual reality around me so that I don't become afraid of or discouraged by temporal difficulties. Help me to trust you more throughout each day and use every situation I face to bring me into a deeper awareness of who you are. Lord, I want to know you and the fellowship of your sufferings, being conformed to your image (Philippians 3:10).

Amen.

RECOGNIZE YOUR POWER TO CHOOSE

*Although we often have little choice of what happens to us,
we surely have some choice as to what happens in us.*

EVELYN UNDERHILL

Charlene came to her session steaming with anger. "My husband is a methodical perfectionist," she cried. "Everything has to be done his way or it's not right. He's driving me crazy. I've had to submit to this insanity for ten years, and I just can't do it anymore." When I asked Charlene why she stayed in her marriage when she was obviously so unhappy and bitter she said: "I'm a Christian. I *have* to stay."

Charlene lost sight of one of the most important freedoms God gives us—our freedom to choose. In his book *Man's Search for Meaning,* Viktor Frankl said: "We who lived in concentration camps can remember the men who walked through the huts comforting others, giving away their last piece of bread. They may have been few in number, but they offer sufficient proof that everything can be taken from a man but one thing: the last of the human freedoms—to choose one's attitude in any given set of circumstances, to choose one's own way."[1]

Charlene had also forgotten that God gives us the ability to choose our attitude as well as our response toward any given situation. Because Charlene believed she had no choice, she constantly felt victimized by God and her husband. But Charlene *did* have choices. She didn't *have* to submit to her husband or stay in her marriage. Charlene didn't *have* to obey God or believe that his ways were good and right. By losing sight of her power to choose, Charlene robbed herself of the joy that comes from making good and right choices with a willing heart.

Victim Mentality

Many of us get stuck because we really believe we have no choices. Like Charlene, we tell ourselves that we *have* to do something; we have no choice. I remember once discussing this concept with a client. She resented going to work, taking care of her children, cleaning the house, and paying her bills. She was always complaining about her lot in life and constantly felt victimized by the circumstances that she believed were out of her control. After one particularly difficult session I reminded her that she *did* have choices. She didn't *have* to go to work, take care of her kids, clean the house, or pay bills. Instead she *could* choose to stay in bed or quit her job. She could choose to give her children up for adoption or put them in foster care if she resented them so much. She could also choose to file for bankruptcy or renege on her financial obligations and just skip town. These were just a few of the different choices she could make given her situation; did she want to hear some more? She looked at me as if I had lost my mind and said, "I couldn't do that! I'd feel horrible about myself."

She's right, and those choices would be terribly hurtful to her children and irresponsible of her as a person. Yet by believing that she had *no* choice in the matter, she was not able to realize any of the self-respect or satisfaction we gain when we *know* we are making good or right choices. My client lost sight of the fact that she was *choosing* to be a good parent and a responsible person by keeping her commitments. She didn't *have* to make that choice. Plenty of people don't.

Choices and Consequences

Every choice we make, whether good or bad, right or wrong, has consequences. The Bible calls it the law of sowing and reaping. (See Galatians 6:7-8.) In the short term, sometimes the consequences seem insignificant. For example, if I choose to eat a big bowl of double chocolate-chip ice cream after dinner, the worst that could happen is that I might feel sick or maybe gain a pound by morning. Over time, however, if I continually choose to indulge my passion for ice cream, I may have more serious consequences, like significant weight gain and clogged arteries.

At times we don't recognize our power to choose our responses to a difficult spouse. As I stated in chapter 3, we often just react. In the short run, these reactions may not seem to cause any significant damage to our marital relationship, but if repeated over and over again, our behavior may have magnified consequences. Marriage expert John Gottman's research claims that "wives who make sour facial expressions when they listen to their husbands are likely to be separated within four years!"[2] The apostle Paul was not a marriage researcher, but he tells us something similar when he cautions, "If you keep on biting and devouring each other, watch out or you will be destroyed by each other" (Galatians 5:15). Other decisions we make can have significant consequences even in the short run. The writer of Proverbs warns us, "Can a man scoop fire into his lap without his clothes being burned? Can a man walk on hot coals without his feet being scorched? So is he who sleeps with another man's wife; no one who touches her will go unpunished" (Proverbs 6:27-29).

It is important that we not deceive ourselves into thinking our choices (whether they be well thought out or impulsive) do not have consequences both for ourselves and others. Jason was an up-and-coming sales rep for a large multimillion-dollar company. He traveled extensively. One day he casually phoned his wife and told her he was tired of family life. He didn't like the responsibility. He was not coming home and (for the time being) merrily went on with his life. His wife and three children were shattered. His actions were like those of a reckless driver who causes a terrible accident and then speeds away so as not to face the devastation that has been triggered. When we are tempted to make bad or sinful choices, we need to remember that there are always consequences to our choices, not only for us but also for others.

Making Right Choices

As Christians, most of us try to make good or right choices and usually do not live life intentionally making wrong or bad choices. Yet when we do, we may be confused as to why we made that choice, especially when we knew ahead of time that it was sinful or foolish. It is important to understand the various factors that contribute to our decision-making process so we can become more mindful of them and thereby make wiser choices.

Look for the Big-Picture Perspective

In order to make good choices, we must learn to look at life out of two lenses at the same time—the regular and the wide-angle. One of the current hot topics in psychology is *emotional intelligence*. Research has shown that innate intelligence, or IQ, is only one factor in a person's ability to be successful. Emotional intelligence, it turns out, is the greater variable. Good emotional intelligence includes having "self-awareness and impulse control, persistence, zeal and self-motivation, empathy and social deftness."[3]

Recently a television news show reported the differences in emotional intelligence among children. Each child in the study was seated alone at a table in a room with a one-way mirror. Each received a small handful of M&M candies and was told if he or she didn't eat the candy right away but waited, another handful of candies would come later. Then the adult left the room and watched the child's response behind the one-way mirror. It was fascinating to observe the different children's behaviors. Some could hardly wait; once the adult left the room they gobbled up the candy. They demonstrated no ability to wait or to delay gratification. They saw, they wanted, they took, and they ate. Other children sat longingly looking at the candy and then busied themselves with some other distraction, knowing if they could wait, they would get a reward. These children were able to hold the picture of more candies in their mind long enough to say no to themselves for now.

This ability to delay what we want now for something greater later is crucial if we are going to learn to make good choices so that we can act right when our spouse acts wrong. Oswald Chambers tells us, "We must learn to harness our impulses." He goes on to add, "We have the ability to fix the form of our choices either for good or bad."[4] If we are prone to looking at life through the temporal lens only, when our spouse acts wrong, we may choose to withdraw, to scream and yell, to have an affair, or to divorce just because we can only see the now, and the now feels intolerable. This is just the time when we need to draw upon the wide-angle lens of life to get the full picture. In his book *Sacred Marriage*, Gary Thomas asks: "Around which world is your life centered? Your marriage will ultimately reveal the answer to that question. If we have an eternal outlook, preparing for eternity by sticking with a difficult marriage makes much more sense than destroying a family to gain quick and easy relief. Most divorces are marked by the actions of someone running from, at most, a few difficult decades—and for this relief, people are throwing away glory and honor that last for eternity. It's a horrible trade!"[5]

If we only have eyes for now, the pain of a difficult marriage can feel unbearable. The psalmist David experienced the anguish of looking exclusively at the temporal. In Psalm 73 he was distraught because it seemed to him that the good guys were suffering for doing good and that the bad guys were thriving. He says, "This is what the wicked are like—always carefree, they increase in wealth. Surely in vain have I kept my heart pure" (verses 12-13). Many dear saints have diligently tried to honor God in their heart and in their home. Perhaps you are one of them, and your spouse has done some pretty wicked things. It looks as if he or she isn't suffering any consequences for his or her sins; instead, you and your children are the ones who are suffering. Like David, you are tempted to throw your hands up and say, "What's the use? Why do it God's way?" The answer is, *Because God's purposes encompass a bigger picture than you can see right now.* David said, "When I tried to understand all this, it was oppressive to me *till* I entered the sanctuary of God; then I understood their final destiny" (verses 16-17).

Sometimes we can only make the best choices when we look through the widest lens of life, the lens of eternity. The apostle Paul taught us this when he struggled with difficult circumstances. He said: "Therefore we do not lose heart. Though outwardly we are wasting away, yet inwardly we are being renewed day by day. For our light and momentary troubles are achieving for us an eternal glory that far outweighs them all. So we fix our eyes not on what is seen, but on what is unseen. For what is seen is temporary, but what is unseen is eternal" (2 Corinthians 4:16-18).

Remember, Our Choices Come from the Desires of Our Heart

The familiar story of Mary and Martha (see Luke 10:38-42) teaches us something about what contributes to our choices. Jesus and his disciples visited the sisters and their brother, Lazarus. In order to be a good hostess, Martha planned to serve a meal. Picture yourself having important company for dinner. Perhaps your pastor and his family. Maybe a well-known speaker or Bible teacher. How would you respond? Martha's mind immediately went to the task at hand. She prepared her list, figured out everything that needed to be done, and went to work. I can relate to Martha's ways. I used to go all out when company came, cleaning, cooking, and baking. Sometimes—no, most times—I'd get so stressed out and exhausted that by the time my company came for dinner, I couldn't wait until it was over and they went home.

Martha's sister, Mary, didn't respond to Jesus' visit in the same way Martha did. Mary couldn't have cared less about making fancy preparations for her special company. All Mary wanted to do was to listen to Jesus talk, sit at his feet, and enjoy his company. I've always chalked this up to personality differences, but Jesus indicated that Mary's behavior was a choice. But why did Mary choose one way, Martha the other? Perhaps for Mary it was more important to spend her time knowing Jesus, and for Martha it was more important serving him. At first glance we might think that these two choices are equally good, but Jesus definitely preferred one over the other. He said, "Martha, Martha, you are worried and upset about many things, but only one thing is needed. Mary has *chosen* what is better, and it will not be taken away from her."

Martha's choice to prepare an elaborate meal came from her desire to serve, to please others, to do a good job, to be a fine hostess. When the task grew too large, she became frantic and harried. Martha's desires were not wrong or sinful, but Jesus didn't want them to be the central or ruling desires of her heart. They distracted her from the most important thing. Mary, on the other hand, desired to know Jesus. That's all. Jesus said she made the better choice.

A. W. Tozer tells us, "True spirituality manifests itself in certain dominant desires. These are ever-present, deep-settled wants sufficiently powerful to motivate and control the life."[6] Our choices reveal what we love the most, what we fear, what is of ultimate value to us, and what we think we need in life—in other words, our choices expose the dominant desires of our heart. Is our dominant desire to be holy or happy? Is it to know God and glorify him through our lives? Or is it to satisfy ourselves?

Don't Confuse Desires with Temporary Feelings

The desires of our heart reflect something much larger than a temporary emotional state. As we learn to exercise our power to choose, it is important that we understand the difference between desires and emotions. Otherwise, we may make choices based on the wrong thing. On a purely human level, I desire to be a good mother. When my children were babies, never, not once did I *feel* like getting up in the middle of the night to feed them or change their diapers. Yet I faithfully did, without any resentment. Why? I loved them. I chose to act in accordance with my desire to be a good parent and not my temporary feelings of fatigue or irritability. Along another vein, I never *feel* like exercising. In fact, I usually feel just the opposite, but I regularly choose to work out. Why? I exercise because it is consistent with my desire to keep my body reasonably healthy and strong. As I write this page I am staring out the window at the ocean on a beautiful, warm, sunny day. I *feel* like going out to play. My desire is to write this chapter. Which is going to rule me? I choose to write.

Jonathan and Carolyn came to me for marital counseling. Jonathan desired to be a godly man and husband, but he faced a continuous inner conflict. Sometimes Jonathan felt insecure when he believed Carolyn didn't pay enough attention to him. He found himself feeling jealous of any time she spent with her sisters, her parents, and even her colleagues at work. Sometimes these feelings would be so powerful they would overwhelm him, and he would react angrily and treat Carolyn disrespectfully. Although Jonathan desired to be a godly man, he regularly based his choices on how he felt. He wanted relief from the anxiety and pain he was experiencing. Instead of working on improving himself, he sought relief in trying to control Carolyn and the time she spent with family and friends. In order to mature in a way consistent with his deepest desires, he would need to learn how to base his choices on his desires to be a godly man and loving husband, not on the temporary wish to control Carolyn, which came out of his insecure emotional state. He would also need to learn to center himself and his security in God and not his wife, so that he would not be so threatened by her independence.

Recognize the Battle Between Your Competing Desires

In addition to the confusion between our emotions and our desires, the Bible speaks of many different kinds of desires in our heart that can influence our choices. The Scriptures speak of evil desires, deceitful desires, sensual desires, ungodly desires, and lustful desires, all of which come out of our fallen nature. For simplicity, I will categorize these desires as our "sinful desires." We also have many good and legitimate desires, which are part of being created in God's image. We have a desire for beauty, a desire for order, and a longing for justice. As God's image bearers, we also desire intimacy and fellowship with others. We long to be loved and to love, and we desire significance and the ability to have a positive impact on others' lives.

As believers, we also have some nonnatural—in fact, supernatural—desires that God has placed in our heart. Our desire to see his glory and to please him above all else is not common to our sinful natures (1 Corinthians 10:31). Our desires to be a servant, to be humble, to bless our enemies, to love those who hurt us, and to forgive those who mistreat us are certainly not a part of our human capacity; instead, they are elements of God's character that we take on as we mature in our relationship with him. (Ephesians 4 and 5 are a great aid in understanding the battle of desires and the change that is to take place in us as we grow.)

Often we find ourselves in conflict between our competing desires. The apostle Paul experienced this battle when he said: "For to me, to live is Christ and to die is gain. If I am to go on living in the body, this will mean fruitful labor for me. Yet what shall I choose? I do not know! I am torn between the two" (Philippians 1:21-23). Paul struggled between two good desires: the desire to be in the presence of God and the desire to serve God by laboring for him on earth. Paul also experienced the tension between his godly desires and the desires of his sinful nature. He said in Romans 7:21-24: "So I find this law at work: When I want to do good, evil is right there with me. For in my inner being I delight in God's law; but I see another law at work in the members of my body, waging war against the law of my mind and making me a prisoner of the law of sin at work within my members. What a wretched man I am! Who will rescue me from this body of death?" His answer? Jesus!

Jesus himself even wrestled with competing desires. He said, "Father, if you are willing, take this cup from me; yet not my will, but yours be done" (Luke 22:42). Jesus wanted to live, but the greater desire of his heart was to glorify and obey God. For that, he was willing to die.

If we are to learn how to make good choices, we must come back once again to looking at our center. Around what do we orient our life? What is the greatest desire of our heart, the defining sphere of our existence? Who or what do we love the most?

God often brings us to a crisis of faith (usually through the troubles in life) when we must make a choice. Do we believe him and what he tells us we need for life and for our well-being, or do we trust our own selves or the ways of the world? Do we really love him, or have we just been giving him lip service? The way we express love toward God is through trust and obedience. The psalmist declared, "I desire to do your will, O my God; your law is within my heart" (Psalm 40:8). When we trust anything or anyone else *more,* we have not centered our heart in God.

Choose to Surrender Your Will to God

We have nothing to give God that is ours alone except our will. God gives us the freedom to choose, and he loves when we choose to show our love for him by yielding our will to him. Love for God cannot be forced upon us any more than love for our spouse can be. God created humankind with a free will, and we must *decide* whether we will obey his commands to love both him and others. This power to choose, however, is exercised through our will, not our emotions. To understand what God is asking of us, A. W. Tozer explains:

> We need only to know that there are two kinds of love: the love
> of *feeling* and the love of *willing*. The one lies in the emotions,
> the other in the will. Over the one we may have little control.
> It comes and goes, rises and falls, flares up and disappears as it
> chooses, and changes from hot to warm to cool and back to
> warm again very much as does the weather. Such love was not in
> the mind of Christ when He told His people to love God and

each other. We could as well command a butterfly to light on our shoulder as to attempt to command this whimsical kind of affection to visit our hearts.

The love the Bible enjoins is not the love of feeling; *it is the love of willing, the willed tendency of the heart.*[7]

When our emotions are in conflict with our desires, whichever is the stronger will be expressed through our actions. When our desires are in conflict with each other, we can, by exercising our will, choose the more excellent path. "Man is what his 'will' makes him, and sin's seat of operation is in the human will. A person's attitude toward God depends on the simplicity of a personal choice."[8]

The psalms are often the scriptures with which we can most deeply identify because they speak of struggle, sorrow, injustice, heartache, and conflict. The psalmist again and again *chooses* to rise above his circumstances by exercising his will. Here are just a few examples:

> *I will* praise you, O LORD, with all my heart;
> > *I will* tell of all your wonders.
> *I will* be glad and rejoice in you;
> > *I will* sing praise to your name, O Most High.
> (Psalm 9:1-2)

> Even though I walk
> > through the valley of the shadow of death,
> *I will* fear no evil,
> > for you are with me. (Psalm 23:4)

I will extol the LORD at all times;

> his praise will always be on my lips. (Psalm 34:1)

I will watch my ways

> and keep my tongue from sin;

I will put a muzzle on my mouth

> as long as the wicked are in my presence.
>
> (Psalm 39:1)

When I am afraid,

> *I will* trust in you.

In God, whose word I praise,

> in God I trust; *I will* not be afraid.
>
> What can mortal man do to me? (Psalm 56:3-4)

But *I will* sing of your strength,

> in the morning *I will* sing of your love;

for you are my fortress,

> my refuge in times of trouble. (Psalm 59:16)

Because your love is better than life,

> my lips *will* glorify you.

I will praise you as long as I live,

> and in your name *I will* lift up my hands.

My soul *will* be satisfied as with the richest of foods;

> with singing lips my mouth *will* praise you.
>
> (Psalm 63:3-5)

> *I will* walk in my house
>   with blameless heart.
> *I will* set before my eyes
>   no vile thing. (Psalm 101:2-3)

Some folks think that they have no choice whether to submit or yield themselves to God. Much as Charlene believed, they think they *have* to do what God says; much as some victims feel they must yield to a bully or a rapist lest something far worse happen. There is a grain of truth in this thought, because God clearly says the consequences of disobedience are severe (Hebrews 10:31). However, the difference lies in the character and motives of God versus the character and motives of the bully or rapist. God loves you, created you, knows you best, and desires only your eternal good. Much like a good parent who knows what her child needs and what is in her child's best interest, God longs for us to trust and believe him. The opposite is true for the bully or rapist. They are only after gratifying their own sick and sinful pleasures and bringing harm to you.

The Call to Choose

In order to learn, children must choose to listen to their parents. Even more important, they must believe that what their parents are teaching them is right, true, or good. Resistance to truth hinders their ability to learn and grow. Whether you learn to act right when your spouse acts wrong will depend upon what you ultimately choose. Will you choose to listen to God and be teachable and believe what he tells you? Will you choose to obey him? Will you choose to yield yourself to him? Or will you choose your own way, what you think is best?

The Bible contains plenty of examples of individuals who made good choices and of others who made poor choices. We can learn from both types of examples. Eve chose to believe the serpent rather than to believe God. She only considered the immediate moment (the fruit looked good to eat and she wanted it), but the consequences of her choice affected the entire human race (Genesis 3:1-6). Moses "chose to be mistreated along with the people of God rather than to enjoy the pleasures of sin for a short time. He regarded disgrace for the sake of Christ as of greater value than the treasures of Egypt, because he was looking ahead to his reward" (Hebrews 11:25-26). Noah chose to believe God and built an ark, suffering the ridicule of his entire community for a season but saving his family in the long run (Genesis 6-8). Abram chose to believe God, and it was counted unto him as righteousness (Genesis 15:6).

Esau chose to sell his inheritance for a pot of stew. He was living for the moment and made his decision on a temporary felt need—hunger (Genesis 25:29-34). The Israelites chose to believe the ten spies who feared the giants rather than to believe Joshua and Caleb, who trusted God. The Israelites made their choice based on feelings of fear and consequently forfeited the opportunity to go into the Promised Land. Instead, they wandered in the desert for forty years (Numbers 13). David chose to honor his commitment and loyalty as a subject of King Saul, even though Saul sought to kill him. When David had the chance to kill Saul, he chose not to, instead trusting God to deliver him and protect him (1 Samuel 18-24).

Queen Vashti chose to say no to her drunken husband, King Xerxes, when he commanded her to parade her beauty before the people and nobles (Esther 1). As a result she lost her position, but she kept her dignity. Abigail chose to do the right thing and overruled her foolish husband's orders when he refused to feed David's men. She saved her family from disaster and David from sinning (1 Samuel 25).

John the Baptist chose to stand for the truth and lost his head rather than compromise with sin (Mark 6:17-29). Yet Jesus says of John that no human being has ever been greater than he (Matthew 11:11). Judas chose to wallow in self-hatred instead of choosing to repent after betraying Christ. He felt so badly he went out and hanged himself (Matthew 27:3-5). Jesus, the very son of God, chose to leave his heavenly kingdom and live among us. He wanted to show us who God was and what he was like. He chose to suffer and die on the cross so that one day we might live forever with him.

"We can decide to live in response to the abundance of God, and not under the dictatorship of our own poor needs. We can decide to live in the environment of a living God and not our own dying selves. We can decide to center ourselves in the God who generously gives and not in our own egos which greedily grab."[9] When our spouse acts wrong we can:

Choose to LOVE . . . . rather than hate.

Choose to SMILE . . . . rather than frown.

Choose to BUILD . . . . rather than destroy.

Choose to PERSEVERE . . . . rather than quit.

Choose to PRAISE . . . . rather than gossip.

Choose to HEAL . . . . rather than wound.

Choose to GIVE . . . . rather than grasp.

Choose to ACT .... rather than delay.

Choose to FORGIVE .... rather than curse.

Choose to PRAY .... rather than despair.[10]

Moses encouraged the people of God with these words: "Now choose life, so that you and your children may live" (Deuteronomy 30:19).

Dear Jesus,

I want to choose you. So often I say I am yielding myself to you, but if I'm honest, I know I am usually more focused on what I want or need in the moment than on your will for my life. Lord, give me the ability to look through your eternal lens toward the things that really matter and make choices that please you in everything that I say and do. Lord, sometimes it is so difficult to believe you and to trust you fully—especially when everything around me is hard or hurtful. Increase my faith. Help me believe what you tell me is true and good. Keep me from listening to the lies of the enemy who seeks to hurt and destroy me and my family. Lord, each and every day help me remember my power to choose. To choose to believe you rather than to doubt you. To choose to serve you rather than myself. To choose to glorify you rather than to live for the moment. Lord, change the desires of my heart so that everything in my life, including my marriage, reflects that you and you alone are the deepest desire of my heart.

Amen.

SEVEN

CHOOSE TO GROW

The important thing is to view the challenges
of our particular life situation as a platform for growth.

GARY THOMAS

My daughter, Amanda, has been taking piano lessons for nearly thirteen years. For most of those years, I have faithfully accompanied her and sat in on her lessons. I carefully listened to her teacher's instructions so that I could reinforce what she was learning at home. I learned about notes, timing, music theory, music appreciation, and composition. Today I know far more about these things than I ever did before, but I cannot play the piano like Amanda. Why? Because I never took anything I heard and put it into practice. I understand *how* to play the piano. I could even teach someone else some of the concepts. But I cannot personally *do* any of them.

Some of us may not be growing spiritually simply because we don't put into practice the things that God teaches us. Week after week we sit in church under good teaching or attend Bible study. We may have our devotions and understand the principles for spiritual growth. We can even teach others these truths, yet we aren't personally growing. Why not? Because we don't diligently apply what we learn to our circumstances. We know God's truth on an intellectual level, but we find it much harder when we have to actually apply it to our life from the heart.

Often in difficult times we pray for relief instead of asking God to help us *practice* the very qualities he seeks to develop in us. God told the prophet Ezekiel: "My people come to you, as they usually do, and sit before you to listen to your words, but they do not put them into practice. With their mouths they express devotion, but their hearts are greedy for unjust gain. Indeed, to them you are nothing more than one who sings love songs with a beautiful voice and plays an instrument well, for they hear your words but do not put them into practice" (Ezekiel 33:31-32). We must ask ourselves, are we looking for a God who just sings love songs to our heart? When he asks us to put his harder truths into practice, do we conveniently ignore him?

Jesus, too, taught the importance of practicing what he teaches us. He said: "Why do you call me, 'Lord, Lord,' and do not do what I say? I will show you what he is like who comes to me and hears my words and puts them into practice. He is like a man building a house, who dug down deep and laid the foundation on rock. When a flood came, the torrent struck that house but could not shake it, because it was well built. But the one who hears my words and does not put them into practice is like a man who built a house on the ground without a foundation. The moment the torrent struck that house, it collapsed and its destruction was complete" (Luke 6:46-49). Jesus both warned us and encouraged us that if we make it our practice to faithfully apply ourselves to the things he teaches us, then we will have a solid foundation when difficulties come. If not, we will be swept away.

In college there are students and there are auditors. Auditors generally aren't considered *real* students. They come to listen to the lecture but never do any of the assignments or take any tests. Some of us just want to audit our faith. We listen but we don't apply. We grow in knowledge but fail in wisdom (the application of knowledge). This type of religion isn't real faith (2 Timothy 3:1-7). Jesus calls us to be his disciples. "*Disciple (mathetes)* says we are people who spend our lives apprenticed to our master, Jesus Christ. We are in a growing-learning relationship, always. A disciple is a learner, but not in the academic setting of a schoolroom, rather at the work site of a craftsman. We do not acquire information about God but skills in faith."[1]

Trying or Training?

For a long time in my Christian life, I tried to put the things I was learning into practice. I would tell myself that I would try to be more joyful or thankful, more content or self-controlled. I earnestly tried to be more patient and show more love toward others. There were times when I tried harder than others, but ultimately I always failed. I could no more try to do these things and succeed than I could try to run a marathon and finish.

This past year I decided that I needed to start doing more than just walking for regular exercise. I tried running. My body rebelled. It didn't like to run, and I found that when I tried to run a mile, I failed. I could run only for about sixty seconds. Each day I would increase the time I ran until I could eventually run for five minutes without stopping or slowing down. My goal is to train myself to run an entire mile without stopping. I can *try* to run a mile forever but will never succeed, but I certainly can *train* myself to run one.[2]

The same process that we use to train our bodies to become stronger applies to spiritual growth and maturity as well. For example, we have already learned how important it is to think about the right response when our spouse displeases us. However, we must start to train ourselves in what that right response might look like. For some of us it may mean learning to keep our mouths shut tight until we've had a chance to think and to pray about how we want to respond. I've never had a problem with words, and I can hold my own against even the most formidable opponent. I have had to train myself to keep quiet when I want to vent. I have had to discipline my tongue not to say everything out loud just because I'm thinking it. Some things are better left unsaid, and I have learned the hard way that reckless and careless words hurt my husband even if at the moment I feel better. Later I may ask for forgiveness, but even a sincere apology doesn't wipe away the sting of ugly words hurled in a moment of uncontrolled anger.

God never tells us to try to be spiritual, he tells us to *train*. Paul said, "Train yourself to be godly" (1 Timothy 4:7). Jesus taught, "A student is not above his teacher, but everyone who is fully trained will be like his teacher" (Luke 6:40). Do you want to be more like Jesus? Stop trying and choose to start training.

Hardship Often Provides the Training Ground

Most of us, if we are honest, prefer "easy" to "hard." We don't usually volunteer for difficult situations, even if we know that good might come out of it. One year my daughter begged me to let her quit piano lessons. Playing the piano was no longer easy. It had become hard. She was used to being able to whiz through her practice times and still please her teacher. Now the piano pieces were more challenging, and she did not have the skill to breeze through them without careful practice. She was tempted to give up. I wouldn't let her, and by teaching her to persevere through the hard times, she has become an accomplished pianist.

When we first get married, most of us find it easy to love our spouse. Communication flows, and we are anxious to please one another. Sooner or later, the blinders come off, and we begin to see our mate's flaws that we scarcely noticed while dating. What once was endearing now is irritating. Our marriage is no longer easy, and it requires something more from us—something, quite frankly, many of us don't have. At this juncture we can either resign ourselves to suffer through a difficult marriage, call it quits, and find someone else so that it's easy once again, *or* we can choose to grow through the difficulties we encounter. Suffering itself doesn't produce growth. We must choose to allow it to teach us its lessons. "Faith develops out of the most difficult aspects of our existence, not the easiest."[3]

Hebrews reminds us, "No discipline seems pleasant at the time, but painful. Later on, however, it produces a harvest of righteousness and peace for those who have been *trained* by it" (Hebrews 12:11). James agrees when he counsels us to "consider it pure joy, my brothers, whenever you face trials of many kinds, because you *know* that the testing of your faith develops perseverance. Perseverance must finish its work so that you may be mature and complete, not lacking anything" (James 1:2-4). Hardship helps build perseverance.

In order to persevere through suffering, we must train ourselves to live with the conviction that our biggest reality is God's reality, and our truest truth is God himself (1 Timothy 6:19). James echoes this when he tells us that we can actually experience joy in the midst of a difficult situation. How can this be? Because we are looking out of two lenses. We are not only living in the present hardship (which may be painful), but in light of the view offered us by that wide-angle lens, which tells us that something good is happening *in us* while we are in the difficulty. He says if we *know* that (in other words, if we believe that), we can experience an inner joy or calm, even in the middle of a trying situation.

Early in my career I worked as a counselor in a hospital oncology (cancer) ward. I saw many people choose to undergo difficult and painful chemotherapy treatments (this was before they had medication to help with the side effects) because they were hoping for a future. During treatment they would lose their hair, vomit continually, and often get large blisters inside their mouths. No one in his or her right mind would willingly choose to endure such suffering *unless* he or she *believed* something good (restored health) would come out of it.

The apostle Paul also has this view in mind when he talks about training. He says: "Run in such a way as to get the prize. Everyone who competes in the games goes into strict training. They do it to get a crown that will not last; but we do it to get a crown that will last forever. Therefore I do not run like a man running aimlessly; I do not fight like a man beating the air. No, I beat my body and make it my slave so that after I have preached to others, I myself will not be disqualified for the prize" (1 Corinthians 9:24-27). What is our defining goal of life? What are we training for? If our goal is temporal—say, to have a happy marriage or a certain feeling—when we fall short of it, we will be tempted to give up. Instead, God wants us to choose the goal of being conformed to the image of Christ. If we do, we will allow him to use anything and everything we experience to achieve that purpose, *even a difficult marriage.*

How we choose to live our lives is based upon the deepest desires of our heart and what we value the most. In order to be able to act right when our spouse acts wrong, we will need to learn perseverance and to see the big picture—what God might be using in our difficult marriage to teach us.

Keeping Our Eyes on the Goal Keeps Us Headed in the Right Direction

Part of what we have been learning thus far is how to see our life through God's wide-angle lens. "Persistence doesn't make sense unless we live with a keen sense of eternity."[4] When we look through God's lens, he gives us a new perspective. Joseph was sold into slavery by his brothers. He was then put in prison for something he didn't do and was forgotten by those who had promised to help. Joseph had plenty of reasons to be despondent, angry, or bitter. For many years he didn't understand what was happening to him or why, yet Joseph persevered, living with the wide-angle lens tightly fixed to his spiritual eyes. Much later, when God's purposes became clearer to him, he could say, "You intended to harm me, but God intended it for good" (Genesis 50:20).

The dictionary defines perseverance as the ability to "remain constant to a purpose, idea, or task in spite of obstacles."[5] In order for us to develop perseverance in our marriage, it is crucial that we understand the specific purpose or idea to which God calls us to remain true. Many Christians are committed to staying married. No matter how awful their marriage is, they will endure; they will never divorce! Although not a bad idea, this goal falls far short of what God intends. God doesn't command us to be committed to staying married; that is too easy. He requires us to be committed to loving our spouse. That is a whole lot harder than just not filing for divorce. To love my spouse demands much more of me than just putting up with a difficult mate or a difficult marriage. To love my husband means I must pursue him, attempt to engage him, to actively seek to know him and to live my life in ways that are in his best interests. Ouch! How do I do that when I don't feel like it or when he isn't responsive? How do I love when he doesn't give me much love in return? when I am angry? when he has just hurt me? It starts with perseverance—choosing to stay committed to your goal (of loving your spouse, of loving God and glorifying him) no matter what the obstacles. Perseverance is a long obedience in the same direction.[6] "Marriage is a long walk."[7]

Regular Practice Is Part of Training

When good athletes and musicians perform, they make it look so easy. If we were to try to do the same thing without training to do it, we would surely fail. We forget that long hard hours of practice behind the scenes have brought them to the place where they have the skills to perform effortlessly. Training takes time and effort. It takes a disciplined commitment to practice something over and over and over again until we get it right. At an ice rink near my home, I watched a young figure skater attempt to do her first double jump. Over and over again she attempted the feat. She'd jump and fall, jump and fall, jump and fall. I must have watched her do this at least a hundred times. She was practicing, and she was determined to keep at it until she got it right. I admired her tenacity. You see, I, too, was at the ice rink because I wanted to learn to skate better. But when I realized that practicing was going to cost me (it hurt when I fell down), I decided it wasn't worth it. I tried, but I chose not to train. As a result, I never grew in my skating abilities.

The ice skater I watched eventually learned her double jump. She persevered through repeated attempts and repeated failures. She didn't lose sight of her goal, and she trained her body to accomplish her heart's desire. The apostle Paul tells us, "Whatever you have learned or received or heard from me, or seen in me—put it into practice" (Philippians 4:9). Sometimes training in godliness hurts and it isn't fun. We are even tempted to give it up, as I did with skating. Yet God promises that throughout our training, he is shaping our character and the very image of Christ is being formed in our life (Romans 5:3-4; 8:28-29). Are you ready to start spiritual training?

Training in Christ's School for Spiritual Maturity

Training is different from trying. In training, we understand that we are moving toward a goal—sometimes one tiny step at a time until we achieve it. When *trying* something, we usually give up when we don't achieve our objectives immediately. I have a client who runs a yearly marathon. When she starts training, she doesn't try to run twenty-six miles all at once. Her body isn't ready to run twenty-six miles—just yet. She must train her body—her mind, her lungs, her legs, and her feet—with daily practice so that she will be able to run that distance when the time comes.

What does it mean when the Bible tells us to train ourselves to be godly? How do we train ourselves to become more like God? One of the first steps would be to learn what God is like and then imitate him. When I was in grammar school I was not one of the more popular girls. I was jealous of the girls who seemed to get more attention, both from the teachers and from the other kids. Sometimes I would pick out one of the best-liked girls and study her carefully. Then I would begin to copy her. I would try to talk like her, toss my head like her, and dress like her, thinking that if I could be more like her, I, too, would be popular. Although I don't recommend this as a strategy for insecure young girls, this method did give me some training in social skills that I didn't receive from my family and that were necessary to building better peer relationships. Several of the writers in Scripture encourage us to imitate their lives and the lives of others who are godly. (See 1 Corinthians 4:16; Hebrews 6:12; Hebrews 13:7; 3 John 1:11.)

In training ourselves to be godly we must understand that we do it one step at a time through faithful practice in the day-to-day situations God orchestrates for us. In this process we train ourselves to think like God thinks, to see life the way God sees it, and to respond to others as he does. In my marriage, a practice that I found very difficult was saying those six little words, *I'm sorry, will you forgive me?* My pride always wanted to hear my husband say them first, because, of course, in my mind he was more wrong than I was. In order to train myself to ask for forgiveness more readily, I had to learn how God sees my sin and how my sin hurts my husband, not to mention my children. The more fully I am able to grasp my own sinfulness, the more I learn humility, and the pride that keeps my lips locked and heart hard begins to lose its grip. The apostle Paul tells us "to put off your old self, which is being corrupted by its deceitful desires; to be made new in the attitude of your minds; and to put on the new self, *created to be like God in true righteousness and holiness*" (Ephesians 4:22-24).

Training Our Mind to Think As Jesus Thought

Our mind is paramount to this transformation process, because we naturally do not think as God thinks. Some of us spend large amounts of time learning about God or studying Scripture, but our thinking is not really changed. In my college biology class I was required to study the theory of evolution. I learned all about the origin of life and natural selection. I passed the tests and gave the "right" answers, but I never believed any of it. Learning about evolution didn't change my mind or my heart. Part of discipleship training is confronting the head-heart split that many of us have, whereby we have head knowledge but lack heart faith. Recently I gave one of my clients an assignment to begin to confront this split. She had a great deal of Bible knowledge yet lacked spiritual discernment and wisdom. Christianity was something she had been taught, but her personal faith was cold. Her assignment was to read through several passages in the book of James and ask herself this question: *How does what God says compare with what I think? Whose version of reality am I going to believe and trust in? Mine or God's?* This is what she came up with:

What James Says	What I Believe
The Lord is full of compassion and is merciful.	God doesn't give a darn.
The Lord is the Father of lights, with whom there is no variation or shifting shadow.	God is capricious, unreliable.
The Lord gives to all men generously and without reproach.	God sometimes withholds good things.
God cannot be tempted by evil, and he himself does not tempt anyone.	God has evil motives in letting bad things happen to good people.

For another assignment, she reviewed one of the psalms, and this was what she discovered:

GOD IS...

My Thoughts	God's Word Says He Is
uncaring, distant	compassionate, merciful
stingy	generous, gracious
hateful, evil	not tempted, not tempting
unloving, aloof	concerned, compassionate

For this particular client to grow, she will not only need to acknowledge her unbelief, she will also need to repent of it. Paul tells us in Romans 12:2 that we are no longer to be conformed to the way this world thinks but instead are to be transformed by the renewing of our mind. By nature we think lies and falsehood (Jeremiah 17:9; Romans 1:25). God tells us that his ways are not our ways, his thoughts are not our thoughts (Isaiah 55:8-9). As Christians we must train our minds to think differently than our culture teaches us and our fallen nature tells us to think. As we spiritually mature, we are to have the mind of Christ (1 Corinthians 2:16).

Training our thinking has specific application in learning to act right when our spouse acts wrong. Isaiah 48:17-18 says, "I am the LORD your God, who teaches you what is best for you, who directs you in the way you should go. If only you had paid attention to my commands, your peace would have been like a river, your righteousness like the waves of the sea." In order to implement the very things we have been talking about, we must believe that God's ways are right and good. We must also train ourselves to think about our marriage from his perspective. For example, the apostle Paul tells us, "Whatever is true, whatever is noble, whatever is right, whatever is pure, whatever is lovely, whatever is admirable—if anything is excellent or praiseworthy—*think* about such things" (Philippians 4:8).

Are we training our mind to focus on what is good and right about our marriage, or do we tend to zero in on all the things we don't like or can't stand about our spouse? As we learned in chapter 2, thinking truthfully about what is going on is crucial to accurately interpret life. If we train ourselves to see our present difficulties as opportunities for training and practice in spiritual maturity, then it's likely we won't be so discouraged when our spouse isn't just what we want him or her to be. Or perhaps we won't be so quick to seek a sinful means of relief from the pain of a difficult marriage. Training ourselves to look at life through God's lens is crucial for our spiritual growth and our ability to then choose to respond to difficult situations as Jesus would.

Training Our Heart to Respond As Jesus Did

The Bible has a great deal to say about our heart. Jesus longs for us to love God more than anything else. Intellectual agreement with Christian principles is not what pleases God. He desires our heart—our whole heart. We will never be able to act right when our spouse acts wrong if our heart is not centered in God and what he wants. Many of us may try to act more loving or more forgiving, but we need to remember that our responses to life come out of our heart. Jesus said, "For out of the heart come evil thoughts, murder, adultery, sexual immorality, theft, false testimony, slander" (Matthew 15:19). If our heart is not right, our actions won't be either. Jesus teaches us that we are to love God with *all our heart* and with *all our soul* and with *all our strength* and with *all our mind* and that we are to love our neighbor as ourselves (Luke 10:27).

Jesus had a God-centered heart. More than anything else, Jesus loved the Father and desired to please him. How do we train our heart to love God more than we love anything else? We love what most impresses us. Jesus was most deeply impressed with God the Father. One of my life passages is Psalm 86:11-13. It says: "Teach me your way, O LORD, and I will walk in your truth; give me an undivided heart, that I may fear your name. I will praise you, O Lord my God, with all my heart; I will glorify your name forever. For great is your love toward me; you have delivered me from the depths of the grave." God's love is great toward us. We can only love him when we begin to recognize how much he has loved us. As we do this, we choose to yield ourselves to God for his purposes and his glory.

The next time you face a difficulty in your marriage, begin to train your heart and mind to yield to God, just as Jesus did. When Jesus was contemplating his betrayal and his death, he said: "Now my heart is troubled, and what shall I say? 'Father, save me from this hour'? No, it was for this very reason I came to this hour. Father, glorify your name!" (John 12:27-28). Just like Jesus, we need to learn to set our hearts and our minds on things above and not on earthly things (Colossians 3:2). How? By contemplating the glory of God, the beauty of Christ, and all he has done for us.

Learning to Be More Like Jesus Is a Day-by-Day Process

Becoming more and more like Jesus in our homes does not come naturally. We must learn how to do it and then practice it as a part of our daily life. Paul says, "Each of you should *learn* to control his own body in a way that is holy and honorable" (1 Thessalonians 4:4). He also says, "Our people must *learn* to devote themselves to doing what is good, in order that they may provide for daily necessities and not live unproductive lives" (Titus 3:14). Just as the apostle Paul *learned* to be content in every and any situation (Philippians 4:12), and Jesus *learned* obedience in the things he suffered (Hebrews 5:8), we, too, are to *learn* to exhibit godly character through our life's experiences. Some of the things we may need to learn when our spouse acts wrong are patience, forbearance, humility, how to speak the truth in love, how to bless our enemy, and how to pray for those who mistreat us. These things are not easy lessons, and they won't make sense to us unless we are training our mind to think like God and our heart to yield to his will for our lives. Training is not just about learning what the Bible says we should do. Many of us have done that and still haven't been transformed by it. "There is a great market for religious experience in our world; there is little enthusiasm for the patient acquisition of virtue, little inclination to sign up for a long apprenticeship in what earlier generations of Christians called holiness."[8]

To become a Christian we must believe in Jesus; to become a disciple we must grow in our confidence in what he says to the point where it begins to change everything. Do we really believe that God rewards those who live a life of obedience? Do we trust that he is sovereign, good, and in control of all of life's circumstances? Are we not only believing *in* God, but believing God too? Learning to become more like Christ is a day-by-day choice whereby we choose to put off our sinful ways and habits and put on our new ways. It is in faithful practice that these things become a more natural expression of our new nature. Peter tells us that "his divine power has given us everything we need for life and godliness through our knowledge of him who called us by his own glory and goodness. Through these he has given us his very great and precious promises, so that through them you may participate in the divine nature and escape the corruption in the world caused by evil desires" (2 Peter 1:3-4).

Peter exhorts us in this epistle to make every effort to grow. As we do so, certain character traits ought to become evident in us. Just as an athlete builds one skill upon another, we, too, will build greater spiritual endurance as we practice and persevere through the training process. These qualities climax until our character is bathed in love. Most of us believe love to be something we have or don't have, but Peter tells us it is something we acquire as we mature. He tells us, "For if you possess these qualities in increasing measure, they will keep you from being ineffective and unproductive in your knowledge of our Lord Jesus Christ" (2 Peter 1:8).

How to act right when our spouse acts wrong will require us to choose to grow, to make every effort through training and practice to think like Jesus, to center our heart in God and develop the character of Christ within. Gary Thomas advises: "Whenever marital dissatisfaction rears its head in my marriage—as it does in virtually every marriage—I simply check my focus. The times that I am happiest and most fulfilled in my marriage are the times when I am intent on drawing meaning and fulfillment from becoming a better husband rather than from demanding a 'better' wife."[9]

As we learn to think more as God thinks and see life from his vantage point, we will begin to understand why God doesn't always answer our prayers in the way we hope or expect. He sees the end from the beginning and most often, instead of giving us relief, uses situations to build into us Christlike character. This prayer was discovered tucked in the pocket of a Confederate soldier after the Civil War:

> I asked God for strength, that I might achieve;
> I was made weak, that I might learn humbly to obey.
> I asked for health, that I might do greater things;
> I was given infirmity, that I might do better things.
> I asked for riches, that I might be happy;
> I was given poverty, that I might be wise.
> I asked for power, that I might have the praise of men;
> I was given weakness, that I might feel the need of God.
> I asked for all things that I might enjoy life;
> I was given life, that I might enjoy all things.
> I got nothing I asked for but everything I had hoped for.
> Almost despite myself, my unspoken prayers were answered.
> I am, among men, most richly blessed.[10]

God knows our real needs, not just our felt needs. When our spouse acts wrong, God will use the resulting injury, whether big or small, to teach us, to train us, to mold us, and to break us in order that we might become a more perfect representative of him to the world *and* to our spouse.

Dear Lord,

So often I have been lax in my spiritual training. I have tried but not trained myself to be like you. Teach me what you are like so I might show more of your character in my home. Lord, transform my mind so that I might think your thoughts and believe what you tell me. I surrender my heart to you and ask that you help me to love you more. Teach me your ways, Lord, that I might begin to look more and more like you in my responses to others. Give me an undivided heart so that I may be most deeply impressed with you. Guard my heart against anything that would cause me to value you less. Thank you for loving me so much that you put me in difficult situations in order to teach me how to become more like you. Help me to begin to see my marriage differently; not just for my personal satisfaction and happiness, but for my sanctification and growth.

Amen.

EIGHT

CHOOSE TO LOVE

Love must be learned.... Hate needs no instruction.

KATHERINE ANN PORTER

"I'm not in love with you, Paul. I never was," sighed Joanne. "I shouldn't have married you, and I don't want to stay with someone I don't love. I'm sorry, but I just don't have any feelings for you."

Joanne chose to end her marriage because she didn't have that certain emotional and physical attraction to her husband that most people call *love*. My dictionary defines love as a "deep affection and warm feeling for another." It continues by describing love as "the emotion of sex and romance; strong sexual desire for another person."[1] Growing up, I learned from soap operas and romance novels that love is something you fall in or fall out of. Love is a feeling—you either have it or you don't. People joke that someone has been struck by Cupid's arrow, has been bit by the love bug, has fallen head over heels, or has been swept off his or her feet. Love is something that happens to us, and if love is absent in a marriage relationship, there is absolutely nothing we can do to find it or revive it.

Although popular and pervasive, these ideas about love are false. They are myths. Contrary to Hollywood and Harlequin and even the

American Heritage Dictionary, God tells us that love isn't a feeling or an ecstatic emotional experience. It is, as the title of one popular book puts it, a decision. Love isn't something that happens to us, it is something we *choose.* God isn't the only one who tells us this. Psychiatrist Scott Peck says in his best-selling book *The Road Less Traveled:*

> Of all the misconceptions about love the most powerful and pervasive is the belief that "falling in love" is love or at least one of the manifestations of love. It is a potent misconception, because falling in love is subjectively experienced in a very powerful fashion as an experience of love. When a person falls in love what he or she certainly feels is "I love him" or "I love her."

Peck goes on to say, however:

> No matter whom we fall in love with, we sooner or later fall out of love if the relationship continues long enough. This is not to say that we invariably cease loving the person with whom we fell in love. But it is to say that the feeling of ecstatic lovingness that characterizes the experience of falling in love always passes. The honeymoon always ends. The bloom of romance always fades.[2]

Often the bloom starts to fade when we begin to realize that our spouse is not all we thought or wished for, and the stark reality of whom we are married to sinks in. Beth Moore writes of her adjustment to married life, "Then it hit me. I wasn't Barbie. He wasn't Ken. This was no dream. And I wanted my mother."[3] This awakening can become a ripe opportunity for us to mature by *learning* what genuine love is. For the Christian, loving our spouse (as well as loving our enemy) is not optional. We are commanded to learn what this kind of love looks like and how to express it through our lives. Jesus commands us to "love each other as I have loved you" (John 15:12).

Jesus Teaches Us About True Love

In order to learn something, one must be willing. Very little learning can take place with a disinterested or rebellious student. My husband often becomes frustrated with my lack of mechanical and technical abilities. Over and over again he has tried to teach me how to program our VCR or how to correct simple computer problems I encounter, but I never remember what he tells me. Honestly, it's not that I can't learn how to do it. I'm sure I could. It's just that I'm not that interested or motivated. I don't pay close attention when he is teaching me the steps, nor do I ever practice what he tells me in order to remember how to do it. The reason for this is because I don't really *have* to change and learn these things. My husband takes care of them. I suspect if I didn't have him to depend on, I'd be motivated to learn fairly quickly.

Jesus invites us to learn from him. He says, "Take my yoke upon you and *learn from me*, for I am gentle and humble in heart, and you will find rest for your souls" (Matthew 11:29). At times our education feels anything but restful. Learning from Jesus can be plain hard. He thrusts us into a difficult situation or calls us to love a difficult person, and we can't see how this can possibly be good. This thrusting is similar to what a mother eagle does to teach her fledglings to fly by forcing them out of the nest. God may put us or keep us in difficult situations so that we might learn how to love better or to grasp more fully what genuine love looks like.

In order to adequately understand God's definition of love, it is helpful to turn to the two Greek words used for love in the New Testament. (Another Greek word used for love, *eros,* or erotic love, is not found in the New Testament.) The first word, *phileo,* is used numerous times to describe tender affection. Jesus is described as having phileo for the disciple John (John 13:23). God the Father has fond affection or phileo for the Son (John 3:35). Phileo love values and cherishes the object of our affection. We all long to receive this kind of love from others. Sometimes we struggle to give it, especially to those who have hurt us.

The other Greek word for love in the New Testament, *agape,* has a slightly different emphasis. Agape love encompasses warmth and tenderness, but this love is not at all dependent upon the recipient's being desirable or attractive. Agape love is solely generated from the disposition and will of the person choosing to love.[4] For example, when the Bible tells us that God so loved the world (John 3:16), it is speaking of agape love. God, because of who he is (God is love), chooses to lavish his love upon us. How? Scripture tells us that God *demonstrates* his love for us in myriad ways, but the most significant way is that while we were our most unlovable selves, Jesus died for us (Romans 5:8). God *showed* his love through personal sacrifice to meet our greatest need, which was forgiveness. He did this *because* he loved us and wanted us to be reconciled to him forever.

Observing this kind of sacrificial love in action often brings me to tears. Recently my local newspaper featured the story of an elderly man caring for his wife, who was suffering from Alzheimer's disease. The photo captured him gently spoon-feeding her, lovingly wiping her chin. In Robert McQuilkin's wonderful book *A Promise Kept,* he, too, shares his journey of learning to love more deeply in the context of difficult circumstances. He writes:

> My imprisonment [caring for his wife who also had Alzheimer's] turned out to be a delightful liberation to love more fully than I had ever known. We found the chains of confining circumstance to be, not instruments of torture, but bonds to hold us closer.
>
> But there was even greater liberation. It has to do with God's love. No one ever needed me like Muriel, and no one ever responded to my efforts so totally as she. It's the nearest thing I've experienced on a human plane to what my relationship with God was designed to be: God's unfailing love poured out in constant care of helpless me. Surely he planned that relationship to draw from me the kind of love and gratitude Muriel had for her man. Her insatiable—even desperate—longing to be with me, her quiet confidence in my ability and desire to care for her, a mirror reflection of what my love for God should be.
>
> That was the first discovery—the power of love to liberate in the very bondage imposed by unwanted circumstances.[5]

Perhaps as you read this you feel that you, too, are in bondage in a marriage that is less than satisfying, less than happy. Longingly you look for the exit door. Realistically you've resigned yourself to stay. You have one foot in, the other out. As stated in chapter 7, being committed to staying married is far less than God's plan for you. If you've read this far, I'm hoping you will press on to learn how to love when it's hard. Genuine love is not generated by feelings, although our feelings may be involved. It is a love that must be learned.

Love's Attributes

Genuine love is not always easy to describe within a marital relationship. What looks like loving behavior in one marriage may be exactly the opposite in another. Sometimes genuine love doesn't look loving and may not feel very loving by the recipient. If we want to learn how to love when our spouse acts wrong, it will be important for us to further explore love's attributes from God's point of view so that we are clear on what is required of us.

Love's Agenda

Roger was losing control. His alcohol use had escalated, and Beth discovered he had withdrawn quite a bit of money from their joint savings account. Some nights he wouldn't come home. Other nights he would call in sick and not go to work. Beth was beside herself with fear and worry. When I suggested to her that she might need to execute the bolder forms of tough love in order to help Roger, she shrank back and said, "I could never do that. I love him too much."

Beth thought she was acting lovingly by putting up with Roger's behavior. Her "loving" actions, however, had her own interests in mind, not Roger's. Beth was afraid to speak honestly with her husband and confront Roger for fear he'd get mad and leave. She needed him and didn't want to lose him.

In our misunderstanding of what genuine love is, sometimes we smile and affirm women like Beth for their perseverance and *great love* for their confused, addicted, or rebellious husbands. We pray that they will be able to continue to endure and bear up well under suffering. However, if genuine love is defined by actions that are directed toward another person's good, let's think for a moment of what was in Roger's best interests. Beth's husband didn't need her to continue to indulge his behaviors; he needed her to confront them. By saying nothing, Beth showed that she didn't love Roger *enough* to risk losing him. Her passivity regarding her husband's behavior was motivated by fear, not real love, even though her patience and forbearance may have looked loving. This is a difficult concept for many of us to grasp. Our emotions are so powerful they can often deceive us into thinking that we *are* acting in another person's best interest when our real motives are more self-serving. Beth was well intentioned but misguided.

Genuine love always has an agenda that acts in the ultimate bests interests of the beloved. "Agape is concerned with the good of the other person."[6] God sacrificed his Son for our good, so that we might be reconciled to him. Scott Peck defines love as "the will to extend one's self for the purpose of nurturing one's own or another's spiritual growth."[7] Although I don't know Peck's spiritual commitment, I think he has captured the essence of what constitutes genuine love. Beth extended herself, but not for the purpose of nurturing Roger's spiritual growth or even her own for that matter. Therefore her actions were more self-serving than loving. The Bible tells us that self-seeking behaviors never define genuine love (1 Corinthians 13:5).

The Scriptures also tell us that love's purpose is to build another person up to his or her God-given potential. It is to bring restoration to a wounded soul and reconciliation to a broken relationship. Love means doing what is good for the other person, not simply being nice. Sometimes love is hard and takes a tough stand. To love a spouse who is engaging in sinful and destructive behavior, we may need to implement radical and sometimes drastic action. If you think that this step might be necessary in your marriage, please seek the advice of a professional Christian counselor or your pastor on how you might best do this. Whenever that kind of action is required, Dan Allender and Tremper Longman caution us in their excellent book *Bold Love:* "Bold love is not reckless or cruel. It is not beating up another in the name of sharing or intervention. *Bold love is courageously setting aside our personal agenda to move humbly into the world of others with their well-being in view, willing to risk further pain in our souls, in order to be an aroma of life to some and an aroma of death to others.*"[8]

Love's Actions

Even when we believe our agenda is for the good of our spouse, we must watch our methods. George became enraged whenever his wife, Jennifer, contradicted him, especially in front of their children. In his fury, he forced his wife to stand in front of their three teenage daughters while he scolded her for being a rebellious and unsubmissive wife. He warned his daughters that worse would happen to them if they chose to follow in their mother's footsteps. When confronted by his pastor on these abusive tactics, he said, "I am acting in love and for all of their best interests." George was deceived. God's Word never endorses sinful behavior in order to teach anyone a lesson, even if, in our opinion, that lesson is necessary or in his or her best interests. George wasn't nurturing his family's spiritual growth; he was crushing it with his sinful and disrespectful behaviors. Genuine love is always accompanied by loving actions. The apostle John says, "Let us not love with words or tongue but with actions and in truth" (1 John 3:18). If George wanted to learn to act right when his wife contradicted him, he would need to look at what her behavior brought out in him (see chapter 2) before he would be able to lovingly confront her.

Hillary grew increasingly tired of her husband's selfishness. In her own hurt and anger she informed Todd that she was filing for divorce. Todd broke down. "Why are you doing this to me?" he sobbed. "I love you so much." Todd was inconsolable over Hillary's decision to end their marriage. He couldn't understand why Hillary found it difficult to believe that he really loved her.

Throughout their ten-year marriage, Todd rarely showed much interest in things that mattered to Hillary. He often worked late, played hard with the guys, and spent money whenever and wherever he wanted, despite Hillary's pleas to purchase a home, spend time as a family, or allow her to complete college. Todd couldn't be bothered with Hillary's needs. He was too busy living as a single person with the perks of married life. Now his world was coming apart at the seams, and he was crumbling.

Do not be misled by calling powerful emotions real love. Todd's feelings for Hillary, although I'm sure they were genuine, were not love. Love is active, not passive. His actions were not loving, nor were they directed toward Hillary's best interests or spiritual growth. Todd's entire lifestyle actually demonstrated the opposite of love. For the most part they were selfish and self-centered. Todd's strong feelings for Hillary were set into motion when he feared losing her. We might better define these emotions as feelings of dependency, not genuine love. That is why it is so important that we not rely on certain feelings to define what love is. In order to act right at this juncture, Todd will need to learn to love Hillary and demonstrate that commitment with loving actions. Whether Hillary gives him an opportunity to learn to love her will be Hillary's chance to also act right. Up to this point, she has allowed her legitimate anger over Todd's actions to harden into bitterness, and she, too, is responding sinfully.

When we understand that genuine love is best defined as loving actions motivated by the express purpose of doing whatever is in the best interests of our spouse, then we show love in many ways, depending upon what our spouse needs (I'm speaking of real needs, not felt needs) at the moment. When our spouse acts wrong, choosing how to love him or her requires much wisdom, prayer, and discernment. What does our spouse need? To experience grace and forgiveness? For us to live with him or her in an understanding way and forbear, knowing that we, too, are full of weakness and sin? Maybe this time we need to hold our spouse accountable for what he or she has done. Or perhaps we need to honestly and gently confront his or her destructive behavior and set boundaries. We can easily see that loving our spouse when he or she is acting wrong isn't a simple choice. Nor may we always feel very loving at the moment. That's why we must understand the nature and purpose of genuine love. It is volitional, not emotional. God even commands us to love our enemies. By commanding this, God doesn't expect that we feel fond affection for an enemy. But he knows that with his power working within us, we can choose to act in the best interests of our enemy with an attitude of humility and gentleness, regardless of our emotions at the time.

Love's Attitude

We would commit a grave error if we believed that genuine love involves just doing the right thing. Genuine love comes from our heart, but we must understand again that a loving heart has more to do with our mind-set than any specific emotional feeling. Our heart embraces a way of thinking about life, our self, our marriage, and our spouse that is reflected in our behaviors toward him or her. For example, behaviors that look loving—such as doing favors for your spouse, helping him or her accomplish tasks around the house, cooking nice meals, or buying gifts—may be done with a totally selfish agenda and superior attitude. These actions would not reflect genuine love but manipulation: *I'm doing these so-called loving actions in order to get something from my spouse or to feel good about myself.* The apostle Paul tells us that our attitude should be like Christ's (Philippians 2:5) and that we should "do nothing out of selfish ambition or vain conceit, but in humility consider others better than yourselves" (Philippians 2:3).

I struggle to embrace the heart of Christ consistently in my marriage. Sometimes I act lovingly and with good purposes, but my inner attitude stinks. I can either be haughty or full of self-pity. Both come from my pride. When we are full of haughtiness, we always think we are *more* right (or *right*eous) than our spouse and may make the terrible mistake of trying to take the speck out of his or her eye while being blinded by our own sinfulness. There is no gentleness or grace in the process—only a haughty arrogance that seeks to scold, correct, or demean another person—all for his or her own good, of course! I pray that if you find it necessary to confront your spouse on his or her inappropriate or sinful behavior, you will be careful to examine yourself first. Galatians 6:1-3 gives us specific instructions for handling some-one who is caught in a sin. Paul tells us that first we need to understand that restoration is always the goal. When we restore something, whether it is an old home or an antique painting, we don't take a bulldozer approach. We do it gently, thoughtfully, and carefully.[9] Our heart attitude must be one of humility as we see from Paul's words: "If any-one thinks he is something when he is nothing, he deceives himself" (Galatians 6:3).

Another obstacle to genuine love is the self-pity that captures our heart. Here we may try to act right or loving toward our spouse, but we resent *having* to do so. The motivation to act right or have certain lov-ing actions is not coming from within (from our heart); rather, it is coming from without. We feel pushed or pressured to act more loving from our church, family, or friends, but we have no desire (or internal mind-set) to learn to love or bless our spouse. We may perform loving actions with a hollow heart. When we are wrapped up in self-pity, we forget that love is a decision and that good (growth and maturity, not to mention joy) comes from following God and choosing his ways of responding during hardship.

Lest you think that genuine love is devoid of any emotion and is just a grit-your-teeth-and-do-it kind of thing, let me assure you that nothing could be further from the truth. Peter calls us to "love each other deeply, because love covers over a multitude of sins" (1 Peter 4:8). Genuine love has emotion to be sure (see 1 Peter 1:22-25), but it is generated, sustained, and maintained by our will and by God's power, *not* by emotions. Loving behavior, just like selfish behavior, flows from our heart. Loving actions are an outward response to an inward heart attitude of servanthood and humility. Scripture tells us that our love must be sincere (Romans 12:9). In other words, if our heart isn't in the right place, our actions will not be genuine. Yet so often when we don't feel loving, it is difficult to engage our will to act loving without feeling like a hypocrite. How can our love be sincere when our emotions are lacking?

Remember when we talked about the difference between desire and feelings in chapter 6? Our desires come from the deepest place in our heart, but they are much broader than just emotions. What are the deepest desires of your heart? Is it to be happy? To be "in love"? Is it to be left alone or to have someone love you? Each of these desires, although not wrong in and of itself, is more self-oriented than God-oriented. God wants the deepest desire of our heart to be to love him with all our heart, all our soul, all our mind, and all our strength and to love our neighbor as our self. Our actions will quite naturally flow out of the desires of our heart. When our desires are God-centered—in other words, to love and to please him—our love is genuine, not hypocritical, even if loving emotions are absent.

Over the span of a marriage, genuine love embraces many different emotions. At times we will experience incredible joy and intense pleasure, great fondness and affection in loving our spouse. At other times our heart will literally ache with sadness, hurt, or confusion. To be certain, marriage is definitely enhanced when the more positive emotions are present, and we ought to be careful to regularly nurture positive feelings within our own heart and mind toward our spouse. In Titus, the older women are instructed to train the younger women to love their husbands (Titus 2:4). The word for love in this context is *phileo*, meaning fondness. Positive feelings are something that come and go in a marriage, but they can be learned and they definitely can be rekindled if they have died. However, even when feelings are absent or tend toward the more negative for a season, our love can be sincere when our heart's desire is to humbly serve our spouse's best interests.

What is the opposite of real love? It is not hate. It is prideful selfishness, self-centeredness, and self-protectiveness. It is reflected in our refusal to act on behalf of our spouse's best interests because it will cost us too much. We are either too full of self-love and self-pity or too gripped by fear to move out of our inner sphere and into his or hers.

How Can We Love?

Simply stated, we can love because we are loved. Perhaps not by our spouse, but we are fully and completely loved by God. Therefore, he enables us, empowers us, and equips us to love well. Oswald Chambers says, "The knowledge that God has loved me to the uttermost, to the end of all my sin and meanness and selfishness and wrong, will send me forth into the world to love in the same way."[10] The apostle Paul cries out that the love of Christ controls him. It changes everything. (See 2 Corinthians 5:14-19.) I so enjoy Eugene Peterson's ability to capture the passion of Scripture in his translation *The Message*. He writes: "Watch what God does, and then you do it, like children who learn proper behavior from their parents. Mostly what God does is love you. Keep company with him and learn a life of love. *Observe how Christ loved us. His love was not cautious but extravagant.* He didn't love in order to get something from us but to give everything of himself to us. Love like that" (Ephesians 5:1-2).

Love like that! That is so different from what our world teaches us about love. Jesus' love was a sacrificial love. It was an extravagant love. It was given to meet our needs, not to give him a warm and fuzzy feeling. He gave love to those who didn't want it, and he gave his love even though we didn't deserve it. That's the kind of love that is necessary if we are to learn to act right when our spouse acts wrong. John tells us, "This is how we know what love is: Jesus Christ laid down his life for us. And we ought to lay down our lives for our brothers" (1 John 3:16). This kind of love is costly because it involves dying to ourselves.

I find that Christians are often confused on what "dying to self" really involves. Sometimes we act like martyrs within our marriage, suffering under all kinds of inappropriate and sometimes abusive behavior, thinking that this means dying to self. It is never wise or godly to sacrifice our self in order to give our spouse more license to sin (gamble, abuse drugs, abuse us or our children, etc.). I think most martyrs, if given the choice, would have fled their situation if they could have. Friends of the apostle Paul helped him escape when he discovered that some people were plotting to kill him (Acts 9:23-25). God does not prohibit us from using wise judgment to flee a situation that is dangerous to our well-being. He does not ask us to sacrifice our lives in order to permit someone to continue to sin against us. That is not what the Scriptures teach when they tell us we must learn to die to ourselves. Dying to self means that we let go of (or die to) our old, immature, and sinful ways and grow to become what God has made us to be—like him. Therefore, like him, we are called to sacrifice our lives for the *good* of another. We see this in action when a person chooses to jump into an icy pond to save a drowning child or chooses to rescue someone from a burning building, risking his or her own life to save another. Jesus said these selfless, sacrificial acts are done with the purpose of doing good for the other person (John

15:13). The other person's welfare (in these instances, physical safety) is put ahead of one's own, even at the cost of one's very own life.

Our love for one another, especially for our spouse, is to be like that. We are willing to sacrifice ourselves, our needs, our desires, our wants, and our dreams for our spouse's good. Beth was reluctant to deal with her husband's drinking problem because she said she loved him too much to confront him. In order to love Roger, she would need to die to herself (her fears of being abandoned, her fears that he would reject her) and love her husband boldly and sacrificially for his good. Proverbs 31 tells us that one quality of an excellent wife is that she brings him good and not evil. What would be good for Roger in this situation? Was it in his best interests to ignore his problem? Or, as spiritually minded husbands and wives, when we are aware our spouse is caught in a sin, should we not try to restore him or her?

What would genuine love have looked like in Todd and Hillary's marriage? How might Hillary have learned to love Todd and acted in his best interests, not her own, when she felt frustrated over his selfishness? It certainly wouldn't mean to continue to indulge his immature and selfish ways. Yet divorcing Todd and breaking up their home wasn't the right way to love Todd either. The mark of true love is sacrificing our self for our spouse's good (as God defines his or her good), not just to keep the peace or to stay married. Hillary might have learned to set boundaries that minimized some of the impact of Todd's behavior on the family. She also may have set into motion some consequences for his choices that may have awakened him to the possibility of needing to mend his ways. For us to love in these *sacrificial* ways, we must work to maintain our wide-angle view of life. Sometimes loving our spouse in a way that is best for them may cost us a lot—in Hillary's case it may cost her the right to seek her own temporal happiness and the right to be loved as she desires. John Piper encourages us to remember: "A Godward life is lived with a constant view to the reward of eternal fellowship with God. This Godward hope is the power that unleashes sacrificial love (Colossians 1:4-5)."[11]

How do we learn to love our spouse, especially when he or she acts wrong? Jesus "does not call us to do what he did, but to be as he was, permeated with love. Then the doing of what he did and said becomes the natural expression of who we are in him."[12] Gary Thomas says: "If we view the marriage relationship as an opportunity to excel in love, it doesn't matter how difficult the person is whom we are called to love; it doesn't matter even whether that love is ever returned. We can still excel at love. We can still say, 'Like it or not, I'm going to love you like nobody ever has.'"[13]

Love encompasses a loving agenda demonstrated by loving actions and bathed in an attitude of humility. It can move through a home in powerful ways through the humble and gentle actions of a lover who has his beloved's welfare in mind, no matter what the cost. Since genuine love begins with a heart that is willing to obey God and desires to love and please him, it offers us freedom from dependence upon certain emotional feelings in order to love well.

Let us continue to learn how to act right when our spouse acts wrong by looking at some of the more specific ways we can *demonstrate* genuine love when our spouse acts wrong.

Dear Lord,

I need you to teach me this kind of love. Sometimes I want to learn it; at other times I resist you. Help me to put my total trust in you. Your ways are always good, and your methods are for my good. I think of the song that says, "Melt me, mold me, fill me, use me." So often I pray to be used in my home, but I don't want to be melted and molded first. But you can't use me if I am hard-hearted, stiff-necked, and filled with resentment and bitterness. So, Lord, melt me. Make me soft so that I am moldable in your loving hands. Fill me with the Holy Spirit so that you can use me to love my husband (wife) better than any other person can. Jesus, please teach me how to express your love toward my husband (wife). Thank you for giving me my spouse to love. I give myself to you. Empty me of me, my self-righteousness, my self-pity, my selfish ways, and instead fill me up with you.

Amen.

NINE

GIFTS OF LOVE

Love is something more stern and splendid
than mere kindness.

C. S. LEWIS

No one loves to receive presents more than I do. Unfortunately, sometimes we can't fully appreciate a gift we've been given if we don't recognize its true value. When my husband and I were engaged, we received one such gift. One day a big box from a fancy department store was delivered to my home. Anxious to see what it was, I ripped the box open and found inside a royal blue, satin-lined, velvet bag. Nestled within the cushy pouch was a glass bowl. I thought to myself, *What do I need with another big bowl?* My mother gasped and said it wasn't just any bowl; this was a very special bowl, a *Baccarat crystal* bowl. My twenty-three-year-old mind didn't appreciate such an extravagant and beautiful gift. I wasn't alone. Neither did my fiancé, who was slightly older but none the wiser in his esteem of prized crystal. To my mother's horror, we promptly took the bowl in its velvet pouch back to the department store and used the money to buy each of us a new pair of ski boots for our honeymoon. Today, we both wish we had kept the bowl.

Like that wedding gift, sometimes the ways in which we love our spouse when he or she acts wrong are not valued or appreciated, but that in no way diminishes the value of the love given. Just as I was unable to appreciate fine crystal, our spouse may be shortsighted or have different ideas of what he or she would like from us. As we learn to love our spouse well during difficult times in our marriage or when our spouse is acting wrong, we develop discernment about what our spouse requires most from us. It may or may not be what our spouse *thinks* he or she needs the most or even at all. At one time or another, all of us have received a gift we didn't really want or ask for yet eventually found it to be just what we needed or what was best for us. My friend Georgia shares the story in her book *A Gift of Mourning Glories* of receiving a "gift" that no one wants—breast cancer. Yet after accepting the cancer as a gift, it changed her life. It refocused her priorities, totally rearranged her lifestyle, and deepened her relationship with God. All were a direct result of having received a "gift" she didn't expect and didn't want.

Many people ignore their need for one of life's greatest gifts—the gift of God himself. We merrily cruise through life never contemplating the great price God paid to obtain our salvation. Just because we don't recognize its worth or know our own personal need for God's sacrificial gift, the value of what God has done is not diminished. As we consider the various gifts of sacrificial love that we can give our spouse, it is vital we keep this perspective in mind so we don't expect our spouse to respond to us in certain ways, like with gratitude or repentance, in order for us to maintain our loving posture.

Gifts of Love

Loving our spouse when we are angry or in pain is difficult and may even feel impossible. At times our spouse may seem more like our enemy than a lover or best friend. The kind of love that gives good gifts to undeserving people is not generated out of a human heart. It is God's love, displayed through our human efforts. This supernatural love springs from our love for God and his love for us. As we center ourselves in God, he pours his love into us. Thus we become a channel through which his gift of love is expressed to others, especially our life partner. When our spouse is acting wrong, we may not be able to give him or her our affection, warmth, or companionship very readily. These are the more human forms of love. However, I'd like to suggest some other ways in which we can love our spouse and seek his or her good, regardless of the current climate of our marriage.

The Gift of Acceptance

Acceptance is one of the most difficult concepts with which people struggle in a marriage. In order to love, we must learn how to accept one another's differences and imperfections. Mature love involves a full knowledge of another person, including his or her weak areas. Our challenge becomes learning to love and to accept the person we have married, not the person we thought he or she was or some idealized version of the person. I've heard people say over and over again in counseling, "You're not the person I married!" One husband replied to such a remark, "Oh yes I am. But the person you dated—he was a fake."

When we have difficulty accepting our spouse's imperfections and weaknesses, not to mention his or her differences, it is usually because we have trouble accepting our own limitations and weaknesses also. A perfectionist disdains the imperfect in others as well as himself or herself. God tells us that we are all sinful people who at times act pretty sinfully toward one another (some of us in big ways). Our selfish and thoughtless behavior manifests itself in countless small ways throughout the day. We leave our dirty dishes for someone else to take care of, or we splash water all over the freshly cleaned bathroom sink. We spend too much money on a toy or outfit or bark at our spouse when we're tired or in a bad mood.

Learning to accept our spouse doesn't mean we like a fault we see in him or her, nor does it imply that we resign ourselves to a hopeless situation. True acceptance is merely understanding reality—that we are all creatures in process and that God isn't finished with us yet. One of the books I read recently opens with this statement: "By the grace of God I am a Christian, by my deeds a great sinner."[1] The apostle Paul encourages us to "be completely humble and gentle; be patient, bearing with one another in love" (Ephesians 4:2). Through the gift of acceptance, we choose to put into practice those very words. We acknowledge where our spouse is right now and stop trying to remake him or her into our own image or our version of the perfect partner.

Sometimes we try to play the Holy Spirit in our mate's life. I hope this book will help you to be a better husband or wife, but please understand me: You will *always* make a lousy god. It is God who teaches us acceptance and why it is important. "Accept one another, then, just as Christ accepted you, in order to bring praise to God" (Romans 15:7). The Lord not only sees us as we are, he also sees what we can be. He works with us to bring out our true self, the one that he has created us to be.

Let's look for a moment at the lives of the apostles Paul and Peter. Before he knew Jesus, Saul (as Paul was called before his conversion) was Christ's enemy. But God saw who he could be and touched Saul with the gift of his light, love, and forgiveness, and Saul was forever changed. Peter the fisherman was rough around the edges. He was impulsive and explosive, but Jesus saw beyond that to what Peter the disciple could be. He accepted Peter's weaknesses *and* saw his potential strengths.

Recently one of my clients said to me after giving her husband the gift of acceptance, "Someday I know he's going to be a great husband. Meanwhile, I'll encourage his good points and pray that God will help him change." Her husband was often stubborn and insensitive to her feelings during conflict. She hated these characteristics in him, and they would get into major battles over minor things. After she accepted that he wasn't going to back down from a conflict, she decided she could. That one decision, plus the gift of acceptance, diminished a great deal of arguing between them, and in turn, their marriage improved.

Remember Sheila (chapter 2) who came home from her spiritual retreat and quickly lost all her joy because her husband, Jeff, had left everything undone? Sheila struggled with accepting Jeff's irresponsible behavior. She *acknowledged* the reality of Jeff's weaknesses but didn't really *accept* them. She resented him and tried with all her might to change him. She talked, pleaded, and begged. When that didn't work she tried throwing a fit, threatening to leave, and setting boundaries by not doing any work around the house. Nothing happened, except her marriage got worse and her house got messier. That's when Sheila decided to give Jeff the gift of acceptance. For now, Sheila has chosen to accept her husband's limitations (that doesn't mean she likes them) and look for the best in him instead of dwelling on the things she doesn't like or wishing he would change. Thomas à Kempis said, "Endeavor to be patient in bearing with the defects and infirmities of others, of whatever sort they be; for you also have many failings which must be borne with by others."[2] Sheila understands that she, too, has faults that Jeff has had to live with, and he has not been nearly as critical of her shortcomings as she has been of his.

Sheila still battles bitterness and thoughts of unfairness, but now she trains herself to remember that she has a choice about how she wants to live her life. She has decided she wants to live peacefully, contentedly, and joyfully. Bitterness and resentment are incompatible with those desires. Therefore, she chooses to guard her heart against those emotions, accept who Jeff is for now, and not look for what he doesn't give her. She is also seeking ways to encourage the good she sees in him. By genuinely accepting his weaknesses and failures, she is more open to seeing his strengths.

Sometimes we refuse to accept our spouses for who they are or where they are. We say things like "I can't believe you did that" or "How could you think like that?" Other ways in which we demonstrate nonacceptance is by saying or thinking, "You're stupid for feeling (thinking, behaving) that way." We seem surprised when our spouse acts imperfectly, stupidly, or differently, as if somehow he or she isn't ever supposed to do such a thing. He isn't allowed to ever be weak, different, or separate. She has to think and feel as we do. And of course, when we believe that, we are usually too full of our own pride to see ourselves very clearly.

The gift of acceptance involves much more than merely acknowledging our spouse's weakness or faults. In order for it to be a true gift, we must stop resenting it. We must learn to be emotionally content with our spouse the way he or she is right now, all the while still asking God to mature him or her.

The Gift of Truth

At times in our marriage we do not face reality. We wish for the best in spite of evidence to the contrary. We close our eyes to information that will help us make better decisions. Much like a woman who ignores a lump in her breast, pretending she doesn't feel what she feels, we often pretend that things are fine or that we are fine, when deep inside we know that is a lie.

Harry and Elaine had been married over forty years. They had a rich history together, five children, many grandchildren. Yet Harry kept a secret that Elaine suspected but wouldn't face. He regularly went away for long weekends, saying, "I just need to be by myself for a while." Elaine wanted to believe him and never said a word to him about the gnawing apprehension in her gut. She feared losing him if she made a fuss. One day while packing for another weekend away, she saw him slip his bottle of Viagra into his toiletry case. Harsh reality came crashing down. *Why would he need that if he was going alone?* Elaine fumed to herself. When Harry left the bedroom she angrily replaced his Viagra pills with aspirin. *He would be in for a surprise!* While I do not recommend Elaine's strategy, I commend her for facing the truth. She knew what Harry was up to. Now he would know she knew. Only at that place could they possibly begin an honest dialogue about their marriage and their future. Wasn't their marriage worth trying to protect? In this instance, Harry didn't need Elaine's acceptance of his weaknesses. He needed her to love him enough to confront him with the truth—not only the truth about his weekend jaunts, but the whole truth about what he was doing in light of God's Word.

Sometimes we believe that in order to act like a Christian we always have to feel fine, happy, and unaffected. When we are angry we pretend we are not. When we are hurt we act as if it doesn't bother us. We paste on our smile and close off our soul. We are not honest with ourselves, let alone our spouse. When we do these things, we deny our spouse the opportunity to really know us. We also rob ourselves of the growth that comes from facing our feelings and dealing with them. Everybody loses and our marriage will suffer.

Diane came to counseling because of depression. After getting to know her, we discovered that the root of much of her depression was an unresolved marital problem. Her husband, a non-Christian, enjoyed watching pornography. He regularly brought home videos and magazines and viewed Internet sites that fed him a steady diet of what he thought women wanted and liked. He tried to talk Diane into extramarital affairs and other things that repulsed her. She feared being honest with her husband because she knew he thought she was a goody two-shoes and a prude. She feared if she didn't go along, at least a little, he would turn to someone else.

Diane's husband was acting wrong, yet what was Diane to do? She loved her husband and wanted to enjoy a sexual relationship with him, but not in this way. Diane decided to give her husband the gift of acceptance *and* the gift of truth. Diane accepted that her husband did not share her Christian values or lifestyle. She didn't like his choices to indulge in pornography, but she chose not to resent that he was not a believer. Next, she honestly but respectfully told him not only how she felt, but how she believed the pornography was damaging his ability to discern right from wrong. She believed it was changing him for the worse. Diane acknowledged that although he didn't share her commitment to Jesus, he had always been a moral man. She feared that he was injuring not only their relationship but himself. She reminded him that recently their preteen son had noticed him "watching those dirty movies again," and she asked him if that was what he wanted their son to watch when he got older. Then Diane stopped talking and prayed for the convicting power of the Holy Spirit and his own conscience to work. For now, he is still watching pornography, but at least he is no longer pressuring her to go along with it. Although their marital problems are far from over, Diane's gift of truth helped reverse the downward slide in their marriage a little and also lifted her depression. It is important to remember that Peter instructs wives not to be preachy toward their unbelieving husbands (1 Peter 3). Our walk is always more influential than our talk. However, there are times that, in order to act right when our spouse acts wrong, we must speak the truth, but always in love.

Blurting out angry or destructive feelings is not a gift of truth. We defend our behavior by saying, "I'm just being honest." The gift of truth is always motivated by love. Both Elaine and Diane could have reacted violently against their spouses' sexual sins. Please remember, love always acts in the best interest of our spouse and for the good of the marriage. Telling someone the truth must be for his or her welfare, not so we can feel better or get something off our chest. For both Diane and Elaine, telling their husbands the truth about their sexual sin was the most loving thing they could do. Not to do so would hurt their husbands and hurt their marriages.

The gift of truth is certainly one of those gifts that is not always appreciated as valuable or loving, especially when our spouse prefers to be in denial about the reality of his or her sin and its effects upon others in the family. That is why it is so imperative to keep in mind what genuine, godly love looks like. We give the gift of truth so our spouse can see reality more clearly and, we hope, make better decisions. When a doctor informs his patient that her recent blood work shows a recurrence of cancer, the doctor doesn't enjoy being honest, yet truth is absolutely crucial to the patient's well-being so that she can choose the steps necessary for her treatment. The doctor tells his patient the truth because it is the most loving and compassionate thing he could do. He knows his patient never *likes* hearing this kind of truth. In the same vein, none of us likes it when our spouse tells us something about our behavior or our attitude that we don't want to face. Yet it is very loving and good that he or she would tell us. Why? So that we do not continue to deceive ourselves into thinking that all is well when we are about to fall off a cliff.

In the Old Testament, the Israelites preferred prophets who told them just what they wanted to hear rather than God's truth. They liked it when their prophets told them that their idolatry didn't matter, that all was well, and that they were secure. God, however, in his loving kindness, sent real prophets who told the truth. Judgment was coming if Israel did not repent and change her ways. Sometimes Israel listened, other times not. At times your efforts to give the gift of truth to your spouse will have wonderful results. At other times you will see no change, no repentance. Perhaps you will even be mocked. Remember, God has called you to love your spouse as no one else on this earth will. That may mean suffering under mockery and still speaking truth. I am encouraged by the Lord's words to Ezekiel the prophet: "The people to whom I am sending you are obstinate and stubborn. Say to them, 'This is what the Sovereign LORD says.' And whether they listen or fail to listen—for they are a rebellious house—they will know that a prophet has been among them" (Ezekiel 2:4-5).

The Gift of Kindness

It is clear from the Scriptures that kindness is part of the fruit of the Spirit (Galatians 5:22) and that being kind is one of the very definitions of love (1 Corinthians 13:4). Yet, as with other gifts, we struggle to give the gift of kindness when we don't feel kind or when our mate has hurt us. When our spouse is acting in a way we don't like, most of us react by treating him or her with contempt. However, contempt is the acid that will erode feelings of goodwill in a marriage more quickly than bad behavior. Is that what you want to happen? Remember, God tells us to "not be overcome by evil, but overcome evil with good" (Romans 12:21). Through acts of kindness we are empowered, not overcome.

The last thing that we *feel* like doing is to be gracious to someone who has hurt us. Joan's husband, Adam, was an alcoholic and a drug abuser. He spent more money on his habit then he did on food and clothes for their kids. His drug use was so out of control that Joan finally asked him to move out until he could get help for his problem. He continued careening out of control and sent less and less money for the family. One day Joan heard through mutual friends that Adam was sick with a bad flu bug. Joan went home and cooked up a big pot of soup and delivered it to his apartment. Joan gave the gift of kindness to her selfish and irresponsible husband. She was not overcome by Adam's evil; she was learning to overcome it with good. The kinder Joan was to Adam, the more obvious was Adam's selfishness.

God speaks of kindness as a means of shaming our enemy (Romans 12:20), which may lead to their repentance. In the Scriptures, Joseph was kind and gracious to his brothers in spite of their cruelty toward him. (See Genesis 37-50.) Being kind and gracious doesn't mean you ignore the wrongdoing or pretend it didn't happen. That's like putting your head back into the lion's mouth after he has already bitten you. Being kind toward your enemy means that whatever happens to you doesn't define you. It doesn't shape you or turn you into something evil. Satan's intention is not only to injure you but also to infect you with evil's poison. Joseph's response to his brothers' injustice, deceit, and treachery caused good to defeat evil. He reminded his brothers, "You intended to harm me, but God intended it for good" (Genesis 50:20).

Jesus tells us, "Love your enemies, do good to them, and lend to them without expecting to get anything back. Then your reward will be great, and you will be sons of the Most High, because he is kind to the ungrateful and wicked. Be merciful, just as your Father is merciful" (Luke 6:35-36). We should be kind toward others because we want to be like Jesus, not because they deserve our kindness. We are a representative of the King of kings and Lord of lords. Therefore, our desire is to treat others with kindness and mercy because we are God's ambassadors and his image bearers. Our kindness and mercy doesn't depend upon whether the other person has been good or bad, wrong or right. They are gifts of love, not rewards for good behavior.

Recently one of my clients had the opportunity to practice giving the gift of kindness to his wife, who decided she no longer wanted to be married. She told Clark, "I never should have married you in the first place. We were not meant to be together." Clark was stunned. Brokenhearted and confused, he worked to pick up the shattered pieces of his life and to begin the healing process. During the divorce, his wife asked him to sign some documents so that she would be able to qualify for a loan. Clark could have said, "No, you're the one who wanted this; live with the consequences." Yet he didn't. Instead he decided that the most loving thing he could do for his wife was to extend to her the gift of kindness and help her. She didn't deserve it, but Clark wasn't loving her because she deserved it or even because he felt like it. He gave her the gift of kindness because God had given it to him.

The Gift of Prayer

Scripture says that Jesus continuously intercedes for us. To be more like him, we must also learn to intercede for others. To intercede means to speak on another's behalf or to plead his case. Moses did this in Exodus 33 when God was about to destroy the Israelites for worshiping the golden calf. Interceding for someone who has hurt us is not easy. Much like an injured animal often attacks other animals, hurt people often hurt other people. If your spouse is hurting you, I'm not suggesting that you continue to offer yourself to be bitten, but I am suggesting that you ask God to help you have his perspective and his compassion toward your spouse, thereby empowering you to intercede on his or her behalf.

Prayer is one of the toughest disciplines, especially intercessory prayer, because it is so others-focused. "By means of Intercessory Prayer God extends to each of us a personalized, hand-engraved invitation to become intimately involved in laboring for the well-being of others."[3] What better gift of love? We often pray *about* our enemy, but do we pray *for* our enemy as often?

I'm reminded of Samuel the prophet. After King Saul had just made some pretty big mistakes, Samuel told him, "As for me, far be it from me that I should sin against the LORD by failing to pray for you" (1 Samuel 12:23). In my life, at times I have been so focused on praying for my own needs, whether material, physical, or spiritual, that intercessory prayer gets tacked on at the end—if I have time. Yet Jesus continuously prays for us, and we are to be like him. We can give our spouse the gift of love by praying for him or her in the following ways:

- We can pray for his or her salvation.
- We can pray for his or her growth and spiritual maturity.
- We can pray that he or she gains wisdom and forsakes foolishness.
- We can pray for the conviction of God and the moral pressure of the Holy Spirit to fall upon our spouse.
- We can pray for his or her eyes to be opened and to see the truth.
- We can pray that those who interact with our spouse would speak the truth to him or her.
- We can pray that our spouse would desire to know God or to know him better.
- We can pray that he or she would desire to be a better husband (wife) or father (mother).

Leanne Payne, in her book *Restoring the Christian Soul,* describes a process of praying for our enemies. In it she concludes with instructions she received from the Lord regarding this matter. He told her: "Pray for the health, the wholeness, of your enemies. Pray for the salvaging of all that is good, beautiful, and true within them. I do a great work, one that will amaze you. Be at rest now from all that besets, offends, attacks—love, write, pray, live in peace in My Presence. Enter the timelessness of My joy and peace."[4]

James, too, encourages us to stick with praying for our spouse by reminding us that "the prayer of a righteous man is powerful and effective" (James 5:16).

The Gift of Forgiveness

Forgiveness is the oil that smoothes over the rough spots as two people struggle to become what God calls them to be. When we keep score on marital wrongs, love is impossible. Although some excellent books have been written on the subject of forgiveness, I still find in my counseling practice a common misunderstanding of what it is. When I asked one client how he will know he has forgiven his wife for her adultery, he replied, "When I don't hurt anymore." Getting past the emotional pain caused by someone who has hurt you is a reasonable goal, but it is not a prerequisite for forgiveness. In fact, it was while Jesus *was* in pain that he forgave those who abused him saying, "Father, forgive them, for they do not know what they are doing" (Luke 23:34). Forgiveness doesn't remove the hurt or the consequences sin has inflicted upon its victim. Sometimes the lifelong consequences are worse than the original sin.

Susan wasn't honest with her husband about how much debt they were in. She had started her own business just a few years earlier, and the expenses were much greater than she had ever anticipated. Instead of sharing that burden with Danny, Susan kept it to herself and tried to resolve her household cash flow problems by taking cash advances on all the new credit-card offers she received. When the creditors finally started calling the house because of unpaid bills, Danny hit the ceiling. Although it wasn't easy, eventually Danny *decided* to forgive Susan for her deceit and pride even though he still *felt* hurt and angry. They had to file for bankruptcy. They lost their home and Susan's business. If Danny had waited until he felt no more anger or pain before he forgave Susan, their marriage may not have survived. The consequences of Susan's deceit were devastating and would impact their lives for years.

Extending the gift of forgiveness doesn't guarantee an absence of pain. Neither does it imply an automatic restoration of the relationship. Sometimes we confuse forgiveness and reconciliation. Forgiveness is something we can offer because of who we are. God tells us we are required and empowered to forgive because we have been forgiven, not because the other person deserves our forgiveness or has even asked for it. In fact, it is often the person who has hurt us the most who never asks us for forgiveness. They are not sorry, or they simply don't care. Forgiveness means choosing not to cling to our right for justice or vengeance. We cancel the debt the offender owes us. In order to be able to do this, we must free our heart from the bitterness and resentment we often feel when someone wounds us.

Although love covers a multitude of sins (1 Peter 4:8), *reconciliation* of the relationship at times depends upon the genuine repentance of the one who has sinned. When we sin, God eagerly desires to forgive us, but our relationship with him is broken until we repent. In order to return to a right relationship with God, we must acknowledge our sin, turn away from it, and seek his forgiveness. We must extend the gift of forgiveness to those who have hurt us, but for true reconciliation to take place, repentance and forgiveness must work together. Part of Susan's repentance involved cutting up all the credit cards, allowing Danny to handle the checkbook, and being accountable for all her expenditures. The restoration of their marriage relationship involved both Danny's *decision* to forgive and Susan's *repentant* heart and behaviors, leading to eventual reconciliation.

Forgiving someone is not in our nature as fallen human beings. Justice and revenge come more naturally. We can only truly forgive someone if we learn *how to do it* from the great Forgiver himself— Jesus. Part of seeing what God is up to in our life when our spouse acts wrong requires our understanding that God teaches us *how* to become more like Jesus through the process of being wounded. For how can we ever learn how to forgive if no one ever hurts us?

There is wonderful freedom in knowing that we do not have to react to a painful wrong either by shutting down or by retaliating. As we grow in our relationship with Christ, we become a reflection of who he is *in* us rather than a reflection of what others have done *to* us. "We will be sinned against and we will be hurt. When that happens, we will have a choice to make: We can give in to our hurt, resentment, and bitterness, or we can grow as a Christian and learn yet another important lesson on how to forgive."[5]

The Gift of Consequences

The gift of consequences may not seem like a gift at all, especially from the perspective of the one receiving it. Yet when given with the right attitude, the gift of consequences can surprise the receiver with life-changing results. Often we hear, "If you've really forgiven me (or, if you really love me), you won't make me suffer the consequences."

Before implementing the gift of consequences we must first understand its purpose. The intent is not to be reactionary or punitive. Establishing consequences should be a well thought-out, prayed-out course of action based on the specific wrongdoing. Consequences should be constructed in order to communicate to our spouse: *This kind of behavior or action is not acceptable, and I will not continue to act as if it does not matter that you do this.*

Shelly was a neatnik. She worked hard to make sure everything was always picked up before she went to bed. John, her husband, took a more casual approach to life. He often would leave his dirty clothes right where he took them off, usually in the middle of the floor. This would drive Shelly crazy. In order to act right, Shelly could make one of several choices. She could choose to give John the gift of acceptance and just pick up his clothes and consider it no big deal in the scheme of things. She tried that, but she found herself resenting his lack of consideration for her hard work around the house. So she decided to give him the gift of consequences—no more resentment, no more bitterness, just consequences. One day she said, "You know, honey, I'm sorry for always nagging you about picking up your clothes. I don't want to be that kind of wife anymore." John's ears perked up, and he nodded in agreement. Shelly continued. "In order for me not to feel resentment, though, I'm going to need to make some changes. Whatever doesn't make it into the hamper won't get washed. You'll have to do your own laundry if you choose to continue leaving it all over the floor." John's smile began to fade. He wasn't sure he liked this new approach. John preferred nagging to facing the chore of doing his own laundry, but after only a week of the new Shelly, John knew she meant it. He began to pick up his clothes and put them in the hamper.

Often consequences come in painful forms. Pain warns us to stop doing something. In college I had a friend who was a paraplegic. She had been injured in a horseback-riding accident and had no sensation from the waist down. One day while she was shaving her legs she realized she had forgotten to turn on the cold water. When she pulled her leg out of the sink, her foot was covered with second- and third-degree burns. God gives us the nerves in our body that respond to pain, like scalding water, in order to warn us: Stop! Take your foot away immediately! When these nerves don't work, we are at higher risk for greater injury. In some circumstances, we may need to implement painful consequences as a way of preventing our spouse from inflicting further harm. If you are considering this gift of love, please seek the guidance of a qualified third party for additional counsel and wisdom. In our own emotional pain, we often cannot think clearly and may overreact, calling it merely a gift of consequences rather than admitting it is something more severe. This gift of pain is most often given as a last resort, only after many other attempts have failed to help our spouse to change his or her hurtful or destructive ways.

For example, as difficult as it was for Tim, he finally began to accept that his wife, Audrey, was a chronic liar. She lied about where she spent her time. She lied about where she spent the family money. She even lied about whom she talked to on the phone. For a long time Tim tried to rationalize Audrey's behavior. "She is just careless. She forgets. She isn't good with details." Yet time and time again, he caught her in bold lies that she refused to admit. One of the gifts of love that

Tim gave Audrey after coming to acknowledge the truth was the gift of painful consequences.

Tim began by refusing to cover for her lies, to make excuses for her with the children, or to pay the bills she had run up. In this way, Audrey would have the opportunity to experience the pain of her choices and begin to look at herself honestly. Tim hoped Audrey would come to her senses and see her need to repent. Whether or not she chose to change would be totally up to Audrey.

At other times, separation may be implemented as a severe consequence for certain sinful behavior. As a Christian counselor I do not say this lightly. Yet at times this is the only gift of love that convinces a spouse to consider his or her destructive behaviors seriously. In the book of Hosea, Hosea let Gomer experience the consequences of her adulterous ways. Her life deteriorated to the point where she was eventually sold as a slave. Hosea showed great love and forgiveness to her by bringing her back and restoring her as a wife. (See Hosea 1–3.)

The kinds of situations that warrant this type of drastic action, in my professional opinion, are domestic violence, chronic adultery, and drug, alcohol, or other dangerous addictions that severely impact home life. These are serious marital sins, highly destructive not only to a marriage but also to the welfare of children who witness or experience such behaviors. Most of the time, those who are involved in these kinds of sins will not acknowledge the problem until they personally experience the painful consequences of their choices.

Sometime ago I met with a pastor's wife who was severely depressed. Beth felt desperate, confused, and isolated, and she had contacted me as her last resort. She didn't know what to do, but suicide seemed like her only option. Her husband, the senior pastor of a large church, was charming in the pulpit but physically and emotionally abusive at home. She could not talk to him. Telling him the truth would have resulted in a slap—or worse. She and her children lived in dread between outbursts. The worst part was that no one knew, and Beth doubted whether anyone would even believe her. She hinted about the fights once to a mutual pastor friend; he advised her to go home and be more submissive. If she told someone everything, perhaps she would be believed, but then what? Would she and her husband be forced out of the church? How and where would they live? No easy options presented themselves.

There are so many variables in each instance of domestic violence that it is difficult to generalize the best way to deal with it. But there is no doubt about one thing: Abuse is sin and a very serious sin at that. Beth's husband was caught in the trespass Paul speaks of in Galatians 6: Those who are spiritual are to try to restore such an offender. What would that look like in Beth's case?

I talked with Beth about implementing the gift of consequences. To help her do this, I involved several different people from her Christian community who would act as a support system for her and as truth bearers to her husband. Together they went to her home, respectfully but firmly confronted her husband with the allegations, and moved Beth and the children to a safe place. Her husband was outraged! "How dare you come into my home and accuse me of these things?" he bellowed. Beth's supporters encouraged him to get the help he needed; until he did, his wife and children would stay separated from him. At first he refused. But when he came to realize that they were not coming home anytime soon, he began to repent. Within six weeks he was involved in personal counseling. Last I heard, Beth and her husband had reconciled, but it took a long time and involved a lot of hard work.

If you are in a situation where your husband or wife is involved in addictive, adulterous, or abusive behavior, please seek some expert Christian counsel on what is the best course of action for you, your spouse, and your children. Your safety is paramount, and there are times when separating—especially in an abusive situation—could actually increase the chances of your being physically harmed.

Pain gets our attention and warns us to stop doing something. The gift of consequences, sometimes painful consequences, is at times the most loving thing you can give your spouse in order to get him or her to stop, even if for just a minute, and examine his or her behavior. If your spouse begins to admit the problem, he or she will probably need outside help to change it. This can be a long process, but you can demonstrate your love by acting in your spouse's best interests.

———❦———

As we learn to give these kinds of love gifts, we will be stretched in ways that may take us way outside our personal comfort zone. Much like my Baccarat crystal bowl, these gifts of love may cost a lot and be totally unappreciated or devalued. Yet when given from a pure heart with no strings attached, they can powerfully communicate to our family our commitment to loving our spouse and protecting our marriage.

Thus far we have looked at why we should learn to act right when our spouse acts wrong. We have learned a lot about how to do it and why we should, but I want to encourage you that there is more. There are great benefits *for you* when you learn these lessons. Contrary to popular opinion, you *can* be a happy person even if you're in an unhappy marriage.

Dear Lord,

Sometimes I doubt my motives when I give gifts of love to my spouse. Help me to want my spouse's good and not to want relief or to prove a point or to get even. This kind of love is only possible when you are at the center of my life and are the deepest desire of my heart. Lord, so often I fall short of love. I live for the moment and lose sight of the bigger picture. I forget that you use every situation in my life, even the most painful ones, to bring forth Christ's character in me. Help me to remember, Lord, what I am created for—to love you and become more and more like you.

Amen.

TEN

THE BLESSINGS
OF ACTING RIGHT

Now that you know these things,
you will be blessed if you do them.

JOHN 13:17

One of the hardest days of my life was the day I got a phone call from my younger sister Pat. She was due to give birth to her fourth child any day. I had been anxiously awaiting the news from afar, as she lives in the Chicago area and I live in Pennsylvania.

When I answered the phone, all I heard were heart-wrenching sobs. Something terrible had happened, but I could not make out her words between her wails. The only thing I heard was the bottom line: The baby within her womb was going to die at birth. They were inducing labor immediately. I made arrangements to fly to Chicago that morning.

Her labor was long and hard—as is the labor of many women—but there was not an ounce of joy in it. There would be no life to look forward to at the end. No child to love and to see grow into a fine human being.

Only deep sorrow at the impending loss of this much awaited child. Once delivered, her only son lived just a few short hours and then died.

In the normal process of childbirth, most women experience great pain, but the pain they suffer is tempered with the anticipation of good news at the end. To suffer with no good news, nothing to look forward to, no life to anticipate, only death as a reward for one's labor, feels unbearable.

Much of this book has been about learning how to "suffer" as a Christian in a marriage that may be difficult. But suffering just for suffering's sake is not to anyone's benefit. To endure pain if it brings no reward or benefit is foolishness. We must have in mind something at the end that makes it bearable. Something that makes the pains of laboring to love and learning to forgive, of choosing to grow and guarding our heart, all worthwhile.

The good news is that wonderful rewards for our hard work await us. There are blessings in learning the hard-fought lessons of spiritual growth and maturity and in learning how to act right when our spouse acts wrong. I began this book by saying that God tells us to learn these lessons because they are good for us. Yet how can this be when we are struggling with a spouse who may be unresponsive to our efforts, or when we remain in a marriage that is unhappy or unsatisfying?

The Lord encourages us through Peter's words that acting right, refraining from retaliating when someone hurts us, and suffering for doing good has rewards (1 Peter 3:8-17). Therefore, let us remind ourselves of the blessings that come from learning to act right when our spouse acts wrong so that we can endure the labor with joy, confident that the ultimate outcome is good.

The Blessings of a Clear Conscience

I always warn my clients that even if their marriage fails and they no longer live with their spouse, they will always have to live with themselves. Therefore, it is crucial to their long-term well-being that they conduct themselves in such a way so that they will have no regrets.

With sadness I have watched many people ignore this important principle. Connie crumbled when she found out that her husband, Donald, was having an affair with her best friend. Donald vacillated in his commitment toward Connie and didn't show a lot of movement toward recommitting himself to her or their marriage. In the midst of his confusion and Connie's deep hurt, she decided to have an affair to get back at Donald, "To let him know how it feels," she said. Her choice to respond to her husband's wrongs with her own affair didn't help matters; it only made them worse. Not only did Connie and Donald eventually divorce, Connie grew increasingly depressed because of what she had done.

Our sin never affects just us. The most bitter of all pain is not the pain of an unhappy or even a broken marriage; it is the pain we bring upon our families by the sinful or foolish mistakes *we* have made. Sin is forgiven but often leaves scars, and some remain for a lifetime. We only have one life to live. We ought, therefore, to think more carefully about the choices we make so that we can minimize our regrets.

Recently I received a card from a lovely lady who had been a client of mine some years back. She had been in a difficult marriage with an abusive husband. For her own safety she needed to separate from him, but she did not initiate divorce proceedings. She waited and watched to see if he would repent and change his ways so that they might be reconciled. Out of respect for her marriage vows, she refused to date other men even though she had plenty of invitations. She prayed for her husband and waited upon God's timing. One year passed without change. Two and three years passed with no change. Then she met a wonderful Christian man. What was she to do? She continued to trust God and waited. Eventually her husband found someone else and filed for divorce, releasing Andrea. In the card, Andrea told me of her recent marriage to that wonderful Christian man. She wrote, "God's timing is perfect. He saved the best for last." Andrea had a clear conscience and was able to enjoy this new relationship without any guilt or regrets.

The Blessings of Self-Respect

The way we respond when someone is acting wrong says a lot about who we are or who we are becoming. Remember, actions flow out of what is in our heart, and self-respect comes when we like who we are. In addition to having a clear conscience, acting right when our spouse acts wrong increases our esteem for ourselves.

Janet wanted to change the way she reacted to her husband's chronic tardiness. He was a workaholic, and although she tried "fixing" him, it didn't work. She became angry when he would promise to be home at a certain time, whether it be for dinner or even a date with her, and then not show up. Whining and nagging only made matters worse. She felt frustrated with him and frustrated with herself. "I don't like the person I'm becoming," she said. "I'm either furious or depressed."

Janet began to accept the reality that she was not going to change her husband. His first love was his job, and there was nothing she could do about it. That being true, she would now have to decide how she was going to respond. After thinking about it, Janet realized that she still wanted to be married, and she wanted to honor God by the kind of wife she was. She reminded herself that Sam had many good qualities, and she stopped rehearsing his faults to herself. In order to act right, Janet decided that whenever Sam was late, she could choose to go about her life and not to wait angrily for him. If they had made plans to go out, she would go and leave him a note, hoping that he would catch up later. When they had company and dinner was ready to be served, she would serve it even if Sam wasn't home yet. As she chose to respond in a way that didn't demean her husband or herself, she felt an increase in her own self-respect. She was no longer angry with herself, because she was responding in a way that was consistent with the kind of person she wanted to be.

In another example, Jason's wife filed for divorce and started making false accusations against him to their children and at their church. Jason made up his mind that no matter what, he was not going to stoop to her level. He was not going to repay insult for insult or evil for evil but would instead overcome evil with good. He treated her with respect when she was disrespectful. He told the truth even when she told lies. He kept his commitments to his children even though she tried to sabotage every visitation he scheduled. In the end, although the situation was a mess and Jason didn't have a lot of hope that it would get any better in the future, Jason felt strong. He knew he had handled himself throughout the ordeal as a godly man, and he felt the internal blessing of self-respect.

The Blessings of Spiritual Maturity and Growth

Recently my husband paid me a compliment and told me that I am not the same person I was when we got married. He reminded me that early on in our marriage I often threatened to leave when I got upset. I couldn't stand conflict and hurt. I would rather shut myself off and end a relationship than stick it out and work through my pain. I wonder what I'd be like now if I had given in to those early impulses to flee? Gary Thomas says: "Marriage helps us to develop the character of God himself as we stick with our spouses through the good times and the bad. Every wedding gives birth to a new history, a new beginning. The spiritual meaning of marriage is found in maintaining that history together."[1]

My husband and I have twenty-five years of history together. We share two children and many memories of both good times and bad. I'm not the only one who has changed and grown in our relationship. He has learned how to communicate with me and is better at sharing his feelings, dreams, and goals. Though the home he came from didn't teach him how to do that very well, marriage has. He has received commendations and is recognized at work for being an excellent communicator and problem solver. Together we have become better people than we would have become alone. We have sharpened each other and shaved off one another's rough spots. We are not perfect, but we are different. We have grown.

Even when growth doesn't occur together or at the same time in a marriage, personal and spiritual growth comes from learning how to act right when our spouse acts wrong. Ruth came to counseling when her husband informed her that their marriage was over. He told her, "I'm coming out of the closet. I'm gay and have found my true soul mate." Ruth was devastated. She became paralyzed with fear and dread. "What's going to happen to me and the children?" she cried. As I got to know Ruth, I discovered a Christian woman who never thought much of her own abilities or strengths. She doubted herself constantly and felt ugly and stupid most of the time. She found it difficult to make decisions, stand up for what was right, ask for what she wanted or needed, or speak her own mind to those closest to her, including her parents and her husband. Through her marital crisis, Ruth began to focus on what acting right would look like in her particular situation. How should she deal with her husband? Begging him to reconsider wasn't working, and she felt like a crumpled up piece of garbage that no one wanted.

Ruth began to grow when she took her focus off her failed marriage and her husband's sin and started to look at herself and her own insecurities. She confronted the internal lies that told her she was a nobody who wouldn't be able to survive if her husband didn't love her anymore. She eventually got a job and found that people enjoyed her and that she was good at what she did. Instead of being crushed by her husband's sin, she grew. Acting right taught her that God's Word has power, that truth is stronger than lies, and that evil is indeed overcome with good. As Ruth grew, instead of trying to win her husband back, she began to speak more honestly with him about how she felt and what was acceptable to her. No, he couldn't take their children to his apartment where he lived with his new friend. No, she wouldn't sign for a home equity loan so he could pay off his debts. Before, she would have given in to his requests because she feared rejection; now she was empowered to act not only in his best interests but also in her own and their children's.

Please take note that what we hope to birth in the process of our suffering makes a difference in our ability to endure. If we hope to invoke a positive response from our spouse, whether it be a heartfelt apology, personal repentance, an improved marital relationship, or a happy marriage, we may end up sorely disappointed and angry. This might cause us to give up in the midst of labor. The child is dead, why persevere? But if we can focus on birthing the character of Christ in us, then we can labor with joy, even in the midst of hardship. We can know that this sanctification process shall birth the lovely image of Christ in us.

The Blessing of Reflecting Jesus to Others

Thus far we have looked at the *internal* blessings of learning to act right—a clear conscience, self-respect, and growth. These are important and valuable rewards, yet there are even more. Other people observe the way we respond during hardship. Our behavior can have a profound effect upon their lives as they watch our responses to many of life's questions. Is God real? Do we trust him? What is faith all about? How do we handle adversity? Does God abandon us in the bad times? Does character matter?

The Blessings to Our Children

As I said earlier, children learn more by what we do than what we say. The choices we make constantly expose them to what we believe is important and how we think about life. These life-defining lessons are not so much formally taught as observed. For example, a child may be told not to be selfish, but what he sees in his parents' lifestyles will have a greater effect on him. Does he see people constantly fighting for their own way, or does he see his parents consistently laying down their rights for the good of others?

I am often asked, "Wouldn't it be better for the children if we divorced rather than fight with each other all the time?" It seems to me that the person asking this question believes there are only two choices: divorce or continue to fight. Another version of the same type of question is, "What am I teaching my children if I stay in a marriage when I don't love their father (or mother) anymore?" Again, the choices seem to be limited to either enduring a marriage that is loveless or ending it. It's pretty clear to me that in both cases the person asking the question has already made up his or her mind which option is better—not only for the children but for him or her.

But God gives us a third option. Stay *and* learn to love. Stay *and* learn to act right and stop fighting. This usually is the best option for both you and your children. Perhaps you are skeptical about what's best for you, but research is undeniably clear about what's best for your kids: Children are better off when their parents stay together, except in cases where there are serious problems of addiction or abuse.[2]

Choosing to act right doesn't guarantee that your marriage will stay intact, but the possibility becomes more likely. However, even if you do all you can and your marriage fails, your children will receive valuable and life-changing lessons as they watch God at work in your life and home. I have a tender spot for single parents, and I know God does too. My own faith has grown as I have witnessed God's taking care of needs, answering prayers, protecting, providing, encouraging, and teaching his ways when a single mom or dad is faithful during one of the most painful times in his or her life. I know that the children in these homes have been specially blessed.

One day I was talking to a counselor-pastor friend of mine. He is a good and godly man, and my respect for him has grown over the years. He shared with me how his mom endured a difficult marriage. He recalled watching her weep at the coldness and unresponsiveness of her husband, his dad. Through his mother's walk, not just her talk, this young boy learned to trust God not just as his Savior, but as his Father and his best friend. Today he has a powerful ministry helping others, and much of it he credits to the faithful example of a God-fearing mother who acted right when her spouse acted wrong.

The Blessings to Your Christian Community

Like it or not, we influence not only our children but others around us. We can all recall the shock and horror we feel when we learn that another Christian has fallen into serious sin. When a Christian marriage fails, it hurts all believers. It rocks our faith in the power of God to change lives. If two believers can't rely on God to learn to love one another, what hope is there for us to learn to practice the other truths of Scripture? When we learn to act right when our spouse acts wrong, we bless our spouse, our children, our self, and we become a blessing to others as well.

Faye was struggling in a new marriage. She had married a widower with three children. Depression wrapped itself around her like a wet blanket. "What if I've made a terrible mistake? I don't know if I can be a good mother to these kids. I don't even know *how* to be a mother!" she cried. Her husband was busy getting back to a thriving business that he had neglected during his first wife's illness and his time as a single parent. He seemed oblivious to Faye's struggles and became defensive when she tried to talk to him. His would quickly reassure her that she was fine and then bury himself in his work. Meanwhile, an elderly woman at their church saw Faye's struggle and began to take her under her wing. Maggie was a radiant picture of the love of Christ for Faye's parched spirit. Faye was surprised to learn that Maggie's husband, Fred, was extremely critical and self-centered. *How had Maggie lived with this man for forty years and yet glowed with the love of Christ?* Faye wondered. *Why hadn't her difficult marriage embittered her?*

Maggie assured Faye that there were no secrets to her inner beauty. "Divorce, dear, just wasn't an option in my day. You either learned to be content with where God had you, or you would shrivel up and get ugly. I had a choice. I would either trust God, or I would trust myself. I chose God, and he has never disappointed me." Little did Maggie realize that her commitment to trust God and act right when her spouse acted wrong would become a lighthouse for other struggling wives when they were tempted to lose their way or become shipwrecked in the mist of marital hardship. Maggie had become a blessing to others *because* of a difficult marriage, not in spite of it. The person who stands for Christ in the midst of difficulty attracts others who want to stand but find themselves wavering or weak. The psalmist tells us, "Commit your way to the LORD; trust in him and he will do this: He will make your righteousness shine like the dawn" (Psalm 37:5-6). We can be a blessing to others by demonstrating the reality of a God-centered life in the midst of our own pain. As we *are* a blessing, we also receive a blessing.

The Blessing to Unbelievers

Everyone who knows us or knows of us observes how we handle our life in both good times and bad. When Paul and Silas were thrown into prison and unfairly treated, they responded by singing praises to God. Can you imagine the surprise of the other prisoners who were listening (Acts 16:25)? Sometimes marriage may feel like a prison. What kind of prisoner are you? What do others hear coming from your heart and mouth? Praises or curses? How you respond when life is difficult affects and influences everyone around you. The apostle Paul learned to be content *while* he was in prison (Philippians 4:11-13).

One of my clients was learning these lessons after making some bad choices in his life. Jared had become involved in a short-lived extra-marital affair because he was discontent with his marriage. His wife wasn't giving him the attention or affection he desired, and he was tempted by another woman who did. Instead of choosing to act right in his marital pain, he acted wrong. The response of his wounded wife was to act right. She examined her own role in their marital break-down, took responsibility for her part, worked on her issues, and chose to forgive her husband. She strengthened her relationship with God and thereby set into motion the healing of their marital relationship. But God wasn't finished with Jared yet. He wanted Jared, too, to act right when things didn't go well for him.

Through a series of events, God put Jared in a low-level janitorial job. He would need to learn how to serve others through the most humbling of tasks, cleaning bathrooms. One day he went to clean a stall as usual and almost vomited. Diarrhea was splattered all over the stall, walls, floor, and seat. The person hadn't bothered to clean up after himself. Jared was disgusted and decided to quit. "Who needs this!" he said to the Lord. Then he heard the still small voice of the Lord say to him, "You do, Jared. Is it too small a thing for you to be my servant?" (See Isaiah 49:6.)

At that moment God was trying to teach Jared how to act right when a stranger acted wrong. Was Jared going to be teachable? Was he going to yield and humble himself to be a servant? In that moment, Jared made a life-changing decision. He decided that he would clean that bathroom the best it had ever been cleaned—and he did.

Jared continued serving the Lord by cleaning his employer's bathrooms until they sparkled. One day he was offered a new job with another company doing different work for higher pay. Jared was thrilled; God was letting him move on. When he went to his boss to give notice, his employer said, "Jared, we don't want to lose you. You have been the best janitor we have ever had in the history of our store. We have been watching you. We don't know how you can stay so happy cleaning bathrooms, but whatever we have to pay you, we want you to stay." They matched Jared's new offer, and Jared decided to stay. As Jared learned to act right and lived it out in his job, it had a profound effect on others watching him. They wanted to know the secret of his joy.

The Blessings of Pleasing God

Too often we are willing to trade these blessings for a bit of temporal happiness or a certain emotional feeling. We tell ourselves that we are getting gypped if we aren't in a great marriage. We forget that the absolute best life we could possibly live is not one in which we are focused on becoming happy and fulfilled but on pleasing God. The mystery of all this is that as we live to please God, we *will* be happy *and* fulfilled. (See Psalm 84:12; Matthew 5:6.)

Paul reminds us, "Whether you eat or drink or whatever you do, do *it all* for the glory of God" (1 Corinthians 10:31). God isn't only glorified in the spectacular moments of our lives. He can be glorified in the everyday, mundane tasks of cleaning toilets, making dinner, or interacting with our spouse and children. We glorify him when, in our heart of hearts, we are most deeply impressed with what he tells us, and we trust him by living out his truths in the daily details of our lives. John Piper reminds us that "God is most glorified in us when we are most satisfied in him."[3]

We please God immensely when we offer him our life to use as he wills. He tells us that this is only reasonable considering all he has done for us (Romans 12:1). Can that sometimes include suffering? Can our suffering be used to glorify God? Yes! When Jesus told Peter of the kind of death he would have, he didn't intend to warn or scare Peter but "to indicate the kind of death by which Peter would glorify God. Then he said to him, 'Follow me!'" (John 21:19).

Are you willing to follow God, to learn to act right when your spouse (or anyone else for that matter) acts wrong, no matter what the cost? That is the question Jesus asks of us when he tells us to follow him. Discipleship costs, but remember: "The cost of nondiscipleship is far greater—even when this life alone is considered—than the price paid to walk with Jesus. Nondiscipleship costs abiding peace, a life penetrated throughout by love, faith that sees everything in the light of God's overriding governance for good, hopefulness that stands firm in the most discouraging of circumstances, power to do what is right and withstand the forces of evil. In short, it costs exactly that abundance of life Jesus said he came to bring."[4]

Each day while doing some writing at the beach, I would take a long walk along the boardwalk. One day an elderly gentleman and I reached the end of the five-mile stretch about the same time. He went all the way to the edge of the pier and touched the pole. Turning he smiled and said, "It makes it all worthwhile when you reach the finish line." His statement reminded me that we must keep our eyes on the finish line of life. Jesus' words "Well done, my good and faithful servant" will make our labors on earth all worthwhile. Shun Fujimoto, after performing his rings routine in the 1976 Montreal Olympics with a broken knee said, "Yes, the pain shot through me like a knife. It brought tears to my eyes. But now I have a gold medal, and the pain is gone." One day we too will no longer have any pain, just joy and blessing upon blessing because we have chosen to live our life in a way that glorified and pleased God.

⚬⚬—⚬⚬

Our life is a story in progress. The book we are living is perhaps one-third, one-half, or even three-quarters done. Our marriage, our family relationships, our home, the way we live, love, think, play, hurt, and react are all in this book for later generations to observe. What kind of story are we writing? Is it the kind of story that we want to tell? So many of us live as if we are passive victims, letting every new wave of circumstance toss us around. We forget that we have a part in authoring our story. We can't control everything that happens to us, but we *can* control how we will deal with it. Are we striving to be the best possible partner to our mate? Let's ask God to help us love our husband or wife better than anyone else ever could, then watch the blessings roll in. Our conscience will be clear, our testimony sound, and maybe, just maybe in the midst of learning how to act right, our marriage will improve. However, the best blessing of acting right is that someday we, too, will be able to say, "I no longer remember the pain, but I have won the race. I have had a life well lived and have heard the precious words 'well done' from my Lord."

And that is more than enough.

Dear Lord,

I want you to teach me to act right when my spouse acts wrong. These are good lessons for me to learn. Help my heart, mind, and will to be fully surrendered to you. Father, keep my enemy Satan from deceiving me into thinking that life is found in pleasure or temporal happiness. Give me the faith I need to trust you with all the difficulties in my life and in my marriage. Help me keep my eyes on the finish line so I don't fall off track. I want to become the person you have made me to be, and I want to learn to love my spouse better than anyone else could. Teach me your ways. And last of all, dear Father, thank you, thank you, thank you that I can know the blessings for me when I trust and obey you.

Amen.

Notes and Acknowledgments

Introduction

1. George Barna, Barna Research Online found at http://
   www.barna.org, statistics on family/divorce (15 November 1999).

Chapter One

1. Gary L. Thomas, *Sacred Marriage: What If God Designed Marriage to Make Us Holy More Than to Make Us Happy?* (Grand Rapids: Zondervan, 2000), 13. Copyright © 2000 by Gary Thomas. Used by permission of Zondervan Publishing House.

2. Gary Thomas, Center for Evangelical Spirituality, newsletter 1 (January 2000).

3. Oswald Chambers, *Prayer: A Holy Occupation,* ed. Harry Verploegh (Grand Rapids: Discovery House, 1992), 62.

4. Wade Horn, "Putting Children Back at the Center of Things," *Fatherhood Today* 4, no. 4 (2000): 3, quoted in "Marriage Proves to Be an 'Elusive' Idea," *Current Thoughts and Trends* (September 2000).

5. Eugene H. Peterson, *A Long Obedience in the Same Direction: Discipleship in an Instant Society* (Downers Grove, Ill.: InterVarsity, 1980), 50.

6. François Fénelon, *The Royal Way of the Cross: Letters and Spiritual Counsels of François de Salignac de la Mothe-Fénelon,* ed. Hal M. Helms, trans. H. Sidney Lear (Brewster, Mass.: Paraclete Press, 1982), 5.

Chapter Two

1. Jeanne Guyon, *Final Steps in Christian Maturity* (Auburn, Maine: Christian Books, 1985), 4.

2. Gary L. Thomas, *Sacred Marriage: What If God Designed Marriage to Make Us Holy More Than to Make Us Happy?* (Grand Rapids: Zondervan, 2000), 21. Copyright © 2000 by Gary Thomas. Used by permission of Zondervan Publishing House.

3. John M. Gottman and Nan Silver, *The Seven Principles for Making Marriage Work* (New York: Crown, 1999), 21.

4. Thomas à Kempis, *The Imitation of Christ* (Springdale, Pa.: Whitaker, 1981), 35.

5. Joe Aldrich, *Secrets to Inner Beauty: Transforming Life Through Love* (Portland, Oreg.: Multnomah, 1984), as quoted in Charles R. Swindoll, *Tale of the Tardy Oxcart* (Nashville: Word, 1998), 364.

6. Oswald Chambers, *Devotions for a Deeper Life,* ed. Glenn D. Black (Grand Rapids: Zondervan, 1986), 71.

7. John T. McNeill, ed., and Ford Lewis Battles, trans., *Calvin: Institutes of the Christian Religion,* vol. 20 of *The Library of Christian Classics* (Philadelphia: Westminster, 1960), 604.

8. Oswald Chambers, *My Utmost for His Highest* (1935; reprint, Uhrichsville, Ohio: Barbour, 1963), 119.

9. Beth Moore, *Praying God's Word: Breaking Free from Spiritual Strongholds* (Nashville: Broadman & Holman, 2000), 59-60. All rights reserved. Used by permission.

10. Oswald Chambers, *Disciples Indeed* (Newton Abbot, England: Oswald Chambers Publications Association, 1955), 69, as quoted by Harry W. Schaumburg, *False Intimacy* (Colorado Springs: Nav-Press, 1997), 142.

11. Chambers, *My Utmost for His Highest,* 211.

12. John Calvin, *Golden Booklet of the True Christian Life: A Modern Translation from the French and the Latin,* ed. Henry J. van Andel (Grand Rapids: Baker, 1952), 68-9.

Chapter Three

1. John M. Gottman and Nan Silver, *The Seven Principles for Making Marriage Work* (New York: Crown, 1999), 2-3.

2. Howard Markman, Scott Stanley, and Susan L. Blumberg, *Fighting for Your Marriage: Positive Steps for Preventing Divorce and Preserving a Lasting Love* (San Francisco: Jossey-Bass, 1994), 13.

3. Jaroslav Pelikan and Daniel E. Poellot, eds., *Sermons on the Gospel of St. John, Chapters 6-8,* vol. 23 of *Luther's Works* (St. Louis: Concordia, 1959), 256-7.

4. Oswald Chambers, *Devotions for a Deeper Life,* ed. Glenn D. Black (Grand Rapids: Zondervan, 1986), 86.

5. Frank Outlaw, "Destiny," quoted in Rob Gilbert, ed., *More of...the Best of Bits & Pieces* (Fairfield, N.J.: Economics Press, 1997), as quoted in Alice Gray, Steve Stephens, and John Van Diest, comps., *Lists to Live By: For Everything That Really Matters* (Sisters, Oreg.: Multnomah, 1999), 69.

Chapter Four

1. John Calvin, *Golden Booklet of the True Christian Life: A Modern Translation from the French and the Latin,* ed. Henry J. van Andel (Grand Rapids: Baker, 1952), 60.

2. R. Laird Harris, Gleason L. Archer, and Bruce K. Waltke, *Theological Wordbook of the Old Testament* (Chicago: Moody, 1980), 931.

3. Oswald Chambers, *Devotions for a Deeper Life,* ed. Glenn D. Black (Grand Rapids: Zondervan, 1986), 92.

4. Warren W. Wiersbe, comp., *The Best of A. W. Tozer* (Grand Rapids: Baker, 1978), 169.

5. Chuck Swindoll, *The Living Insight Study Bible* (Grand Rapids: Zondervan, 1996), 1315.

6. Beth Moore, *Praying God's Word: Breaking Free from Spiritual Strongholds* (Nashville: Broadman & Holman, 2000), 76. All rights reserved. Used by permission.

7. Moore, *Praying God's Word,* 7.

8. Oswald Chambers, *My Utmost for His Highest* (1935; reprint, Uhrichsville, Ohio: Barbour, 1963), 14.

Chapter Five

1. Gary L. Thomas, *Sacred Marriage: What If God Designed Marriage to Make Us Holy More Than to Make Us Happy?* (Grand Rapids: Zondervan, 2000), 114. Copyright © 2000 by Gary Thomas. Used by permission of Zondervan Publishing House.

2. David Steindl-Rast, *The Music of Silence: A Sacred Journey Through the Hours of the Day* (San Francisco: Harper, 1995), 18-9.

3. My pastor, Howard Lawler, gave a series of sermons on Philippians in which he used this phrase to describe the lordship of Christ over our life.

4. David L. Miller, "I Am Enough for You," *Lutheran Woman Today* 12, no. 8 (October 1999): 7.

5. Thomas, *Sacred Marriage,* 24.

6. John Piper, *A Godward Life: Savoring the Supremacy of God in All Life* (Sisters, Oreg.: Multnomah, 1997), 19.

7. Oswald Chambers, *My Utmost for His Highest* (1935; reprint, Uhrichsville, Ohio: Barbour, 1963), 74.

8. Warren W. Wiersbe, comp., *The Best of A. W. Tozer* (Grand Rapids: Baker, 1978), 17.

9. Max Lucado, "Keeping Company with God," *Discipleship Journal,* no. 106 (1998): 25.

10. John Piper, *Desiring God: Meditations of a Christian Hedonist* (Portland, Oreg.: Multnomah, 1986), 55.

11. Wiersbe, *The Best of A. W. Tozer*, 180.

12. For a more in-depth examination of our struggle with idols, refer to chapter 4, "Underlying Idols of the Heart," of my book *The TRUTH Principle* (Colorado Springs: WaterBrook, 2000).

13. Piper, *A Godward Life*, 24.

14. C. S. Lewis, *The Weight of Glory* (Grand Rapids: Eerdmans, 1949), 2.

15. L. M. Miles, "The Eagle Psalm" (1998). Used with permission.

Chapter Six

1. Viktor Frankl, *Man's Search for Meaning: An Introduction to Logotherapy* (New York: Simon & Schuster, 1984), 75.

2. John Gottman, *You Can Make Your Marriage Work* (New York: Simon & Schuster, 1994), jacket.

3. Daniel Goleman, *Emotional Intelligence* (New York: Bantam Books, 1995), jacket.

4. Oswald Chambers, *Devotions for a Deeper Life*, ed. Glenn D. Black (Grand Rapids: Zondervan, 1986), 163.

5. Gary L. Thomas, *Sacred Marriage: What If God Designed Marriage to Make Us Holy More Than to Make Us Happy?* (Grand Rapids: Zondervan, 2000), 110. Copyright © 2000 by Gary Thomas. Used by permission of Zondervan Publishing House.

6. Warren W. Wiersbe, comp., *The Best of A. W. Tozer* (Grand Rapids: Baker, 1978), 112.

7. Wiersbe, *The Best of A. W. Tozer,* 172.

8. Chambers, *Devotions for a Deeper Life,* 14.

9. Eugene H. Peterson, *A Long Obedience in the Same Direction: Discipleship in an Instant Society* (Downers Grove, Ill.: InterVarsity, 1980), 93.

10. Alice Gray, Steve Stephens, and John Van Diest, comps., *Lists to Live By: For Everything That Really Matters* (Sisters, Oreg.: Multnomah, 1999), 215.

Chapter Seven

1. Eugene H. Peterson, *A Long Obedience in the Same Direction: Discipleship in an Instant Society* (Downers Grove, Ill.: InterVarsity Press, 1980), 13.

2. I first heard this distinction between "trying" and "training" on an American Association of Christian Counselors teaching tape by John Ortberg, taped at the 1999 AACC World Conference at Nashville, Tennessee.

3. Peterson, *A Long Obedience in the Same Direction,* 74.

4. Gary L. Thomas, *Sacred Marriage: What If God Designed Marriage to Make Us Holy More Than to Make Us Happy?* (Grand Rapids: Zondervan, 2000), 109. Copyright © 2000 by Gary Thomas. Used by permission of Zondervan Publishing House.

5. *The American Heritage Dictionary,* 3d ed., s.v. "persevere."

6. This is the title of Eugene Peterson's book on Christian discipleship.

7. Thomas, *Sacred Marriage,* 266.

8. Peterson, *A Long Obedience in the Same Direction,* 12.

9. Thomas, *Sacred Marriage,* 101.

10. Alice Gray, Steve Stephens, and John Van Diest, comps., *Lists to Live By: For Everything That Really Matters* (Sisters, Oreg.: Multnomah, 1999), 195.

Chapter Eight

1. *American Heritage Dictionary,* 3d ed., s.v. "love."

2. M. Scott Peck, *The Road Less Traveled: A New Psychology of Love, Traditional Values, and Spiritual Growth* (New York: Simon & Schuster, 1978), 84-5.

3. Beth Moore, *Things Pondered: From the Heart of a Lesser Woman* (Nashville: Broadman & Holman, 1997), 14.

4. Spiros Zodhiates, ed., *The Complete Word Study Dictionary: New Testament* (Chattanooga: AMG International, 1992), #26, 878; #5368, 75-6, 965.

5. Robertson McQuilkin, *A Promise Kept* (Wheaton, Ill.: Tyndale, 1998), 32-3.

6. Henry Cloud and John Townsend, *Boundaries in Marriage* (Grand Rapids: Zondervan, 1999), 117.

7. Peck, *The Road Less Traveled,* 81.

8. Dan B. Allender and Tremper Longman III, *Bold Love* (Colorado Springs: NavPress, 1992), 19.

9. I heard Paul Tripp speak on Galatians 6:1 at the Sandy Cove Married Couples Conference in November 2000. He said that if we are to be like Christ and we must confront someone, love is the method, restoration is the hope, and gentleness is the attitude.

10. Oswald Chambers, *My Utmost for His Highest* (1935; reprint, Uhrichsville, Ohio: Barbour, 1963), 95.

11. John Piper, *A Godward Life: Savoring the Supremacy of God in All Life* (Sisters, Oreg., Multnomah, 1997), 20.

12. Dallas Willard, *The Divine Conspiracy: Rediscovering Our Hidden Life in God* (San Francisco: Harper, 1998), 183.

13. Gary L. Thomas, *Sacred Marriage: What If God Designed Marriage to Make Us Holy More Than to Make Us Happy?* (Grand Rapids: Zondervan, 2000), 266. Copyright © 2000 by Gary Thomas. Used by permission of Zondervan Publishing House.

Chapter Nine

1. Helen Bacovcin, trans., *The Way of a Pilgrim* and *The Pilgrim Continues His Way* (New York: Image Books, 1978), 13.

2. Thomas à Kempis, *The Imitation of Christ* (Springdale, Pa.: Whitaker, 1981), 34.

3. Richard Foster, *Prayer: Finding the Heart's True Home* (San Francisco: Harper, 1992), 201.

4. Leanne Payne, *Restoring the Christian Soul: Overcoming Barriers to Completion in Christ Through Healing Prayer* (Grand Rapids: Baker, 1996), 190.

5. Gary L. Thomas, *Sacred Marriage: What If God Designed Marriage to Make Us Holy More Than to Make Us Happy?* (Grand Rapids: Zondervan, 2000), 168. Copyright © 2000 by Gary Thomas. Used by permission of Zondervan Publishing House.

Chapter Ten

1. Gary L. Thomas, *Sacred Marriage: What If God Designed Marriage to Make Us Holy More Than to Make Us Happy?* (Grand Rapids: Zondervan, 2000), 107. Copyright © 2000 by Gary Thomas. Used by permission of Zondervan Publishing House.

2. For more information on the long-term effects of divorce on children, see Judith S. Wallerstein, Julia M. Lewis, and Sandra Blakeslee, *The Unexpected Legacy of Divorce* (New York: Hyperion, 2000).

3. John Piper, *The Pleasures of God* (Portland, Oreg.: Multnomah, 1991), 241.

4. Dallas Willard, *The Spirit of the Disciplines* (San Francisco: Harper Collins, 1991), 263.

ABOUT THE AUTHOR

Leslie Vernick is a licensed clinical social worker with a private counseling practice near Allentown, Pennsylvania. She received her master's degree in clinical social work from the University of Illinois and has completed postgraduate work in biblical counseling, cognitive therapy, and counseling strategies for those who have been abused and those who have abused others. She is the author of *The TRUTH Principle: A Life-Changing Model for Spiritual Growth and Renewal* (WaterBrook) and is an adjunct professor at Philadelphia Biblical University. She is an active member of the American Association of Christian Counselors and teaches in two of their video series: *Marriage Works* and *Extraordinary Women*.

Leslie and her husband, Howard, have been married more than thirty years and are the proud parents of two grown children, Ryan and Amanda.

Leslie is a popular speaker at conferences, women's retreats, and couples' retreats. She loves to encourage and motivate people to deepen their relationship with God and others. If you would like to schedule Leslie for a retreat of conference, contact her at 1-877-837-7931 or visit her Web site at www.leslievernick.com.